YOUNG READER'S EDITION

BROTHER ANDREW

WITH JOHN AND ELIZABETH SHERRILL

Chosen

a division of Baker Publishing Gro
Minneapolis, Minnesota

T0019085

Published by Chosen Books
11400 Hampshire Avenue South
Bloomington, Minnesota 55438
www.chosenbooks.com

Chosen Books is a division of
Baker Publishing Group, Grand Rapids, Michigan

Printed in the United States of America

Library of Congress Cataloging-in-Publication Data
Names: Andrew, Brother, author. | Sherrill, John L. | Sherrill, Elizabeth.
Title: God's smuggler / Brother Andrew ; with John and Elizabeth Sherrill ; abridged by Lonnie Hull DuPont.
Description: Young Reader's Edition. | Minneapolis, Minnesota : Chosen, 2017. | Previously published: 2015.
Identifiers: LCCN 2016036273 | ISBN 9780800798055 (trade paper : alk. paper)
Subjects: LCSH: Andrew, Brother—Juvenile literature. | Bible—Publication and distribution—Europe, Eastern—Juvenile literature. | Missions—Europe, Eastern—Juvenile literature. | Missionaries—Europe, Eastern—Biography—Juvenile literature. | Missionaries—Netherlands—Biography—Juvenile literature.
Classification: LCC BV2372.A7 A3 2017 | DDC 266.0092 [B] —dc23
LC record available at https://lccn.loc.gov/2016036273

Scripture quotations are paraphrases. Andrew read the Bible in Dutch, and during his travels, he and those he encountered translated Scripture into a language they both understood.

Text abridged by Lonnie Hull Dupont

Cover design by Gearbox
Interior illustrations by Tim Foley

23   7 6

CONTENTS

Contents

PREFACE

The events in this book are true. They happened before many of us were born. They happened in places many of us have never seen or may never visit—and they happened to people we don't know.

And yet such stories can be thrilling to read.

After World War II, the victorious Soviet Union (now Russia) imposed Communist regimes throughout Eastern Europe. These countries were known as being behind the Iron Curtain—not a real curtain, but an imaginary curtain separating the free world from Communist nations. Under Communism, citizens living behind the Iron Curtain were not allowed to leave their country without permission. Nobody was allowed to own property, and everyone worked for the government (or the State). If a person wanted to leave or to live a more individual life, that person was likely to be punished.

Communists were atheists—people who believe God does not exist. Faith in God was especially threatening to the regime, because Communism could not have its people more devoted to religion than to the State. So they outlawed worship.

How did Communist regimes enforce this? Sometimes they closed churches. Sometimes they ridiculed believers publicly or took away their jobs or their homes. Sometimes they imprisoned believers, and occasionally, yes, they even killed them.

This meant that people in Communist countries either were frightened into submission or worshiped secretly. Religious reading material was usually outlawed—especially Bibles.

This is important to know as you read *God's Smuggler*. History is part of the book, and of course you can always supplement your history knowledge by using the library or the internet. Look especially for a map of countries behind the Iron Curtain.

But the story is really this: Many years ago, a boy in a small town in the Holland region of the Netherlands wanted to trade in his wooden shoes for excitement. You will read how he grew up in search of adventure, only to make many mistakes in his life. But God used this Dutchman's particular talents—his intelligence, his imagination, his work ethic and his nerve. When our Dutchman decided his life's mission was to serve God behind the Iron Curtain, his life truly had purpose. He became known as Brother Andrew, and he found the adventure he'd always sought.

He also found himself connected to believers around the world—people who loved God but thought their fellow Christians had abandoned them until Brother Andrew showed up with greetings from the outside and, miraculously, with Bibles.

God used Brother Andrew's unique talents to help him become a smuggler for the faith. As you read, think about how God could use your talents—even those that people in your world may not appreciate right now. Keep that in mind.

So let's go meet that adventurous boy in his wooden shoes. . . .

1

Smoke and Bread Crusts

From the time I first put on wooden shoes—*klompen* we call them in the Netherlands—I dreamed of derring-do. I was a spy behind the lines; I was a scout in enemy territory; I crept beneath barbed wire while bullets flew around me.

We kids didn't have any enemies in my hometown of Witte, so we made enemies out of each other. We fought with our *klompen*; any boy who got hit with a wooden shoe just hadn't reached his own fast enough. I remember the day I broke a shoe over my enemy-friend Kees's head. What horrified us both was not the enormous bump on his forehead, but the ruined shoe.

That night my hardworking blacksmith father had to repair my shoe. Already that day Papa was up at five to water and weed the garden that helped feed his six children. Then he pedaled four miles on his bicycle to his job in Alkmaar. Now he spent the evening gouging a little trough across the top of the wooden shoe, pulling a wire through the trough, nailing the wire down on both sides and repeating the process at the heel so that I had shoes to wear to school.

"Andrew, you must be careful!" he said in his loud voice. Papa was deaf and shouted rather than spoke.

In my boyish fantasies there was one family that acted as the enemy—the Family Whetstra.

Why I picked on the Whetstras I do not know. They were the first in our village to begin talking about war with Germany. They were strong Christians. Their God-bless-yous and Lord-willings seemed sickeningly tame to a secret agent of my stature. So in my mind they were the enemy.

Once I passed Mrs. Whetstra's kitchen window as she was putting cookies into the oven of her woodburning stove. Leaning against the front of the house was a new pane of window glass, and it gave me an idea. I picked up the piece of glass and moved stealthily through the lines to the back of enemy headquarters. The Whetstras, like everyone in the village, had a ladder leading to their thatched roof. Off came my *klompen,* and up I went. I placed the pane of glass on the chimney. Then I crept back down the ladder and across the street to watch from the shadows.

Sure enough the smoke backed down the chimney. It filled the kitchen and began to curl out the open window. Mrs. Whetstra screamed, jerked open the oven door and fanned the smoke with her apron. Mr. Whetstra raced outside and looked up at his chimney. The expression on his face as he climbed the ladder was worth it. I chalked up for myself a victory.

Maybe my action fantasies were a means of escaping Mama's radio. A bad heart forced her to spend much of each day in a chair, where her consolation was the radio. She kept the dial on the gospel station from Amsterdam. Sometimes it was hymn singing, sometimes it was preaching; always—to my ears—it was dull. Not to Mama.

We were poor; our house was the smallest in the village. But to our door came an unending stream of needy people who knew that they would be welcome at Mama's table. The cheese that night would be sliced thinner, the soup stretched with water, but a guest would never be turned away.

Thriftiness was as important as hospitality. At age four I could peel potatoes without a centimeter's waste. When I was seven, the potatoes passed to my little brother Cornelius, while I graduated to the responsibility of shining our leather shoes for Sunday. My older brother Ben did the laundry. The only member of the family who did no work was the oldest child, Bastian.

Bas never learned to do the things other people did. He spent the day standing under an elm tree, watching the village go by. Witte was proud of its elms—one for every house, their branches meeting to form a green archway over the road. For some reason Bas never stood beneath our tree. His post was under the third one down. There he stood all day, until one of us led him home for supper.

As the villagers passed his elm tree, they would call to see his shy and wonderful smile. "Ah, Bas!" He heard this so often that he began to repeat it, the only words he ever learned.

Though Bas could not even dress himself, he had a remarkable talent. In our sitting room, as in most Dutch parlors, was a small pump organ. In the evenings Papa would sit on the bench, pumping the foot pedals and picking out tunes from a hymnbook while we sang.

The minute the music started, Bas would crawl beneath the keyboard, crouch out of the way of Papa's feet and press himself to the baseboard of the organ. Papa's playing was full of mistakes; years of wielding a hammer on an anvil had left his fingers thick and stiff. Sometimes he seemed to hit as many wrong notes as right ones.

To Bas it never mattered. He would press against the vibrating wood with rapture on his face. From there, he could not see which keys were played. But all at once Bas would stand up and gently push against Papa's shoulder.

"Ah, Bas," he would say.

Papa would get up, and Bas would take his place at the bench and begin to play. From beginning to end he would play the songs Papa had played that night. But Bas played them perfectly, with such beauty that people would stop in the street to listen. On summer nights when our door was open, a crowd would gather outside. When Bas played, it was as though an angel sat at the organ.

The big event every week was church. Witte was in the polder land of Holland—land that generations of Dutchmen had reclaimed from the sea—and like all villages in the polders was built along a dike. It had only one street, the road leading north and south on top of the dike. The houses were virtual islands, each built on its mound of earth and connected to the road with a tiny bridge spanning the drainage canal. At either end of town were the two churches.

Because of Papa's deafness, we sat in the first pew at our church. The pew was too short for the entire family to sit together, and I would lag behind Mama and Papa and the other children going in first. Then I would walk toward the rear of the church to "find a seat"—usually far beyond the church door. In winter I skated the frozen canals in my wooden *klompen*. In summer I sat so still in the fields that crows would sit on my shoulders and peck gently at my ears.

Somehow I knew when the church service was over and would slip into the building. I listened for comments from the congregation about the sermon, picking up the minister's text, his theme, sometimes even a story.

This ploy was important so that I could discuss the sermon that afternoon with the family. Could I fool my parents into thinking that I had been to church?

I blush to think how seldom I attended church as a child. I blush more that my trusting family never suspected.

By 1939 the Germans were intent on conquest that included the Netherlands. In our house we scarcely thought about it. Bas was sick with tuberculosis. For months he lay coughing. His suffering was horrible to watch.

I remember one day just after my eleventh birthday creeping into the sickroom while Mama was busy in the kitchen. Entering that room was strictly forbidden, for the disease was contagious. But that was what I wanted. If Bas was going to die, then I wanted to die, too. I threw myself down and kissed him again and again.

In July 1939, Bas died, while I stayed healthy as ever. I felt that God had betrayed me twice.

Two months later, in September, our government called for a general mobilization. Now Mama allowed her radio to be used for news.

My sister Geltje stationed herself at the set and shouted information to Papa. "All reserve units are activated, Papa. . . . All private cars are commandeered."

By nightfall, every automobile in the Netherlands was on the road. I watched from under the tree where Bas used to stand. Nobody talked much.

I could not understand why I was drawn toward the Whetstras at this time, but I found myself walking past their kitchen window.

"Good afternoon, Andrew."

"Good afternoon, Mrs. Whetstra."

"On an errand? You'd better have a cookie for energy." She brought a plate of cookies to the window.

Mr. Whetstra spoke up. "Is that Andrew? Out to see the mobilization firsthand?"

"Yes, sir." For some reason I put my cookie behind my back.

"Andrew, you must say prayers for your country every night. We are about to go through a very hard time."

"Yes, sir."

"They'll be here, Andrew, with their steel helmets and their goose step and their hate, and all we will have is our prayers." Mr. Whetstra came to the window and leaned across the sill. "Will you pray, Andrew?"

"Yes, sir."

"Good boy. Now get along on your errand."

As I started down the street, he called after me. "You know, sometimes that old stove of ours smokes something awful. But it's worked fine ever since I got my new window in."

He had known all along. I wondered why he had not told my father. I also wondered about his wanting me to pray. If the Germans came, I planned to do a lot more than pray. I fell asleep that night dreaming of the feats of daring I would work single-handed against the invader.

By April, our country was bombing our own dikes, deliberately flooding land to slow down the German army. Every house except ours, which was too small, held a homeless family from the flooded land.

But the Germans did not come by land. The first planes flew over Witte the night of May 10, 1940, the night before my twelfth birthday. We spent the night huddled together. By day we saw planes and heard them bomb the military airfield four kilometers away.

Then the Germans bombed Rotterdam. The radio announcer wept as he read the release. In one hour Rotterdam disappeared from the earth. The next day the Netherlands surrendered.

Soon a German lieutenant arrived in Witte in a squad car and set himself up in the burgomaster's house. The handful of soldiers accompanying him were older men; Witte was not important enough to rate crack troops.

I really did act out my fantasies of resistance. Many nights I crept barefoot down the ladder from the loft bedroom as two o'clock struck on the town clock. I knew my mother heard me, but she never stopped me. Nor did she ask the next morning what had happened to our rationed sugar. Everyone in the village was amused when the lieutenant's staff car began to give him trouble. Some said there was sugar in the lieutenant's gas tank; others thought it unlikely.

Food ran out in the towns before it did in farming villages. One day that first summer, I loaded a basket with cabbages and tomatoes and walked four miles to Alkmaar. A store there still had fireworks, and the proprietor wanted vegetables.

The proprietor watched as I filled my basket with firecrackers. Then he reached under the counter and brought up a large cherry bomb. "Get home before the curfew," he said.

That night, I slipped out. Four soldiers moved up the street toward our house. I flattened myself against the side of the house as they drew closer. The minute they passed I sped across the little bridge to the dike road and ran to the burgomaster's house. I could have fired the cherry bomb in the lieutenant's doorway while the patrol was at the other end of the village. But I wanted more adventure than that. I was the fastest runner in the village, and I thought it would be fun to have these old men run after me.

The patrol began back down the street. Just before they got to headquarters, I lit the fuse and ran.

"Halt!" I heard a rifle bolt being drawn. I had not counted on guns! As I zigzagged up the street, the cherry bomb exploded. For a moment the soldier's attention was diverted. I darted across the first bridge I could find, raced through a garden and flung myself down among the cabbages. For an hour they hunted for me, shouting to one another. Finally they gave up.

Elated by this success, I began discharging volleys in broad daylight. Once I stepped from hiding straight into the arms of a soldier. In my left hand were firecrackers, in my right, matches. My hands clenched.

I grabbed the edges of my coat with my clenched hands and held it open for the soldier to search. The soldier went over me from my trousers to my cap. When he left, the firecrackers in my hand were drenched with perspiration.

As the occupation dragged on, I tired of my games. In villages near ours people were lined up and shot and houses burned to the ground as the real resistance took shape.

All over the Netherlands men and boys went into hiding in the polders to escape deportation to the forced labor camps in Germany. My brother Ben, sixteen when the war began, went into hiding. For five years we had no news of him.

Possession of a radio became a crime. We hid ours in a space under the sloping roof, and we would crouch there listening to Dutch-language broadcasts from England.

As the Germans grew desperate for manpower, Witte's occupation force was withdrawn. Then came the dreaded *razzia*. Trucks sped into the villages, at any hour of the day or night, sealing the dike road at both ends. Soldiers searched every house for able-bodied men. By age fourteen I

joined the flight of men and boys into the polders at the first sign of a German uniform. We ran across fields, crouching low, and leaped canals, making our way to swamps beyond the railroad. By the end of the war even my deaf Papa was racing to the swamp.

Life became hard. Electricity was reserved for Germans. With nothing to power the pumps, rainwater lay stagnant over the polders. There was no coal, so Witte cut down its elms, including the tree under which Bas had stood.

We were constantly hungry. Crops were commandeered for the battlefront. Our family of six lived on rations for two. We dug tulip bulbs from our garden and ate them like potatoes. But the tulips ran out. Many nights I saw Mama divide her food portion among the other plates. Her only consolation was that Bas had not lived to see this.

Then in the spring of 1945 the Germans left. People wept for joy in the street. But I was running five miles to a Canadian encampment, where I was able to beg a bag of bread crusts.

I brought it home to my family. As Mama gnawed the dry crusts, tears of gratefulness rolled down her cheeks.

The war was over.

The Yellow Straw Hat

Soon after liberation, my sister Geltje told me Papa wanted to see me.

I walked into the cabbage patch, where he was bent over his cabbages. I shouted, "You wanted to see me, Papa?"

Papa straightened slowly. "You're seventeen years old, Andrew. What do you plan to do with your life?"

I wished we didn't have to be so loud. "I don't know, Papa."

"It is time for you to choose a trade, Andrew. By fall I want your decision." He leaned back over his hoe.

I had two months to decide. I knew what I wanted: to break out and find adventure. My prospects were not good. When the Germans came, my schooling had ended in sixth grade.

I took off running across the polders, along the footpaths used by farmers. After five miles, the solution was clear.

There was talk about armed rebellion in the colonies. The Dutch East Indies, recently liberated from Japan, now wanted to claim independence from the Netherlands, too.

That night I announced to the household that I was going to join the army.

The following day I borrowed Papa's bicycle and pedaled to the recruiting office in Amsterdam. Before long I was strutting through Witte in my new uniform. I was going to take back our colonies for the queen, and perhaps get a few of those revolutionaries everyone said were Communists.

Other than my mother, the only people who did not respond with applause were the Whetstras. I walked past their house in my uniform.

"Hello, Andy."

"Good morning, Mr. Whetstra." The sun glinted from my brass belt buckle. "I've joined up. I'm going to the East Indies."

Mr. Whetstra nodded. "Yes, I see. So you're off for adventure. I will pray for you, Andrew. I will pray that the adventure you find will satisfy."

I stared at him, puzzled. What did he mean? Any adventure would satisfy me.

I worked hard during basic training. Some of it took place in the town of Gorkum. Each Sunday I would go to church, because afterward I could count on being invited to dinner. I enjoyed telling my hosts that I had been picked for special commando training in Indonesia.

"Within a few weeks," I would say, "I'll be in hand-to-hand combat with the enemy." Then I would ask if my hosts would consider writing me while I was overseas. Before I left Holland I had seventy names on my correspondence list.

One was a girl I met after church—the most beautiful girl I had ever seen. About my age, slender, with hair so black it had a tinge of blue. I had read about skin as white as snow; this was the first time I had seen it. I timed my exit just right. Snow White was at the door. She introduced herself.

"I'm Thile," she said.

"I'm Andrew."

"My mother wonders if you would like to have dinner with us."

"Very much indeed," I said, and moments later I left with the princess on my arm. I knew this young girl was going to be one of my correspondents and, perhaps, a lot more.

November 22, 1946. It was time to leave my family.

If only I had known it was the last time I would see Mama. But I didn't know. As I was ready to leave, Mama embraced me. Then she gave me her Bible. "Andrew, will you take this with you?"

Of course I agreed. You cannot say no to your mother. I put the Bible in the bottom of my duffel bag and forgot it.

Our transport ship landed in Indonesia just before Christmas. My heart raced with excitement at the heavy tropical smells and the sounds of hawkers on the dock trying to get our attention. I shouldered my duffel bag and struggled down the gangplank into the sun of the dockside. I did not guess that within a few weeks I would be killing children and unarmed adults like those who crowded around me now.

There were hawkers selling monkeys. Each monkey was held by a chain, and many had been trained to do tricks. I was fascinated by these little creatures with their serious faces and stooped to look at one of them.

"Don't touch him."

I straightened up to find myself facing one of my officers. "They bite, soldier."

I withdrew my hand, but I knew I had to have a monkey of my own.

Those of us who qualified were sent to an island for training as commandos. I liked running the obstacle courses: scaling walls, swinging across creeks on vines, wriggling under machine-gun fire. I liked combat training, where we worked with bayonets, knives and bare hands. For some reason the thought never penetrated that I was training to kill human beings.

The day we were flown to the front, I knew instantly I had been wrong about this adventure. Targets were not pieces of paper; they were fathers and brothers like my own. Often our targets weren't even in uniform.

What was I doing? I was more disgusted with myself than I imagined possible.

Then occurred the incident that has haunted me ever since. We marched through a village that was inhabited. We had been in combat daily for three weeks, and the nerves of everyone in our unit were on edge. Halfway through this village we stepped into a nest of mines. The company went berserk and started shooting everything in sight. When we came to ourselves, there was not a living thing in the village. Then I saw the sight that was to send me nearly mad. A young Indonesian mother lay on the ground in a pool of blood, a baby at her breast. Both were killed by the same bullet.

I wanted to die after that. In the next two years I became famous throughout the Dutch troops in Indonesia for my crazy bravado on the battlefield. I bought a bright yellow straw hat and wore it into combat. "Here I am!" it said. "Shoot me!" I gathered around me a group of boys who reacted as I did. We had a motto we posted on the camp bulletin board: "Get smart—lose your mind."

Everything we did those two years was in extremes. When we fought, we fought as madmen. When we drank, we drank until reason left us. We would weave from bar to bar, hurling our empty gin bottles through store display windows.

In the morning, I wondered why I did these things. I turned to my pen pals. I had kept up with everyone I had promised to write. I shared my confusion with some, and they wrote back the same thing: "You're fighting for your country, Andrew. The rest doesn't count."

Thile said more. Thile's letters spoke straight to my own wretchedness. She talked about forgiveness, and there she lost me. My sense of guilt was wrapped around me like a chain, and nothing could ease it.

One day when I was on leave in Jakarta, walking through the bazaar, I spotted a little gibbon sitting on top of a pole, eating some fruit. He jumped onto my shoulder and handed me a section of orange. I laughed, and the salesman came running.

"Sir, the monkey likes you!"

I laughed again. The gibbon blinked twice and then showed me his teeth in what could have been a grin.

So I acquired a monkey. I took him back to the barracks. The boys were fascinated.

"Does he bite?"

"Only crooks," I said.

It was a senseless remark. But no sooner had I said it than the monkey jumped out of my arms, swung along the rafters and landed, of all places, on the head of a guy who had been winning more at poker than averages allowed. He flailed his arms, trying to knock the monkey off his head. The whole barracks was laughing.

"Get him off me!" Jan Zwart shouted.

I reached out my hand, and the monkey ran to me.

Jan's eyes were murderous. "I'll kill him," he said quietly.

So on the same day I gained one friend and lost another.

I had had the monkey a few weeks when I noticed his stomach seemed to be hurting him. I put him on the bed and told him to lie still. Carefully I pulled back his stomach hair. Evidently when he was small, someone tied him with a piece of wire and never took it off. As the monkey grew, the wire became embedded in his flesh. It must have caused him terrible pain.

I took my razor and shaved off the monkey's hair in a three-inch-wide swathe around his middle. The welt was red and angry looking. While the boys in the barracks looked on, I cut gently into this tender flesh until I exposed the wire. The gibbon lay with amazing patience. Even when I hurt him, he looked at me with eyes that seemed to say, "I understand." When I was able to pull the wire away, he jumped up, did a little cartwheel, danced around my shoulder and pulled my hair, to the delight of all—except Jan.

After that, my gibbon and I were inseparable. Whenever I was not on duty in the daytime, I would take him on long runs into the forest. He loped along behind me until he grew tired. Then with a sprint he would dash forward, jump up and cling to my shorts until I put him on my shoulder. We would run miles until I stopped to rest on the ground.

There were monkeys in the trees overhead. My little gibbon would race into the treetops to swing and chatter with the others. The first time this happened, I thought I had lost him. But the minute I stood, there was a shriek in the branches overhead and the gibbon was back on my shoulder.

One day when we got back into camp, I found a letter from my brother Ben. He went on about a funeral. Slowly I realized it was Mama's. Apparently a telegram had been sent but never arrived. I slipped away from camp. I didn't want even the gibbon with me. I ran until my side throbbed in pain.

That week Jan Zwart took his revenge. One evening I came in from guard duty to be met with the news, "Andy, the monkey's dead."

"Dead? What happened?"

"Someone picked him up by his tail and kept slamming him against the wall."

"Was it Zwart?"

The guy would not answer.

"Where's the monkey now?"

"Outside in the bushes."

I found him draped over a branch. But he was not dead. I picked him up and brought him inside. His jaw was broken. A hole gaped in his throat. When I tried to give him water, it ran right out the hole. Jan Zwart watched me, prepared for a fight. But I didn't fight.

Over the next ten days I nursed that monkey day and night. I sewed his throat closed and fed him sugar water. I rubbed his little muscles. I stroked his fur. I kept him warm and talked to him constantly.

Slowly, my gibbon began to eat, and then to crawl about on the bed, and at last to sit up and chatter at me. After two months he was running with me again in the forest.

But he never recovered his confidence in people. He trembled when people were close. Then he wrapped his legs and tail around my arm and hid his head in my shirt.

News came of a major new drive against the enemy. I asked if someone would drive me and my gibbon into the jungle. "I want to let him go and then drive away fast," I said. "Will anyone take me?"

"I'll go."

Jan Zwart. I held his eye for a long time, but he did not blink.

"All right."

As we drove into the jungle, I told the monkey why I could no longer keep him. When we stopped, I put the little gibbon on the ground. His eyes stared into mine with what looked like comprehension. He did not try to jump back into the jeep. As we pulled away, he watched us until we were out of sight.

The next morning, February 12, 1949, our unit moved out. It was a good thing I had let the monkey go when I did. On this mission, a bullet smashed through my ankle, and I was out of the war.

It happened so suddenly. We walked into an ambush, and I was shot in the ankle. As I ran, I suddenly fell and could not get up. My right boot had two holes in it. Blood was coming out of both.

A buddy rolled me into a ditch out of sight. Medics came with a stretcher. They put me on it and began moving me out, crouching low. I still had on my yellow hat. A bullet once went through the crown. I didn't care.

Hours later, I was on an operating table in the evacuation hospital. It took two and a half hours to sew up the foot. I heard the doctors discussing whether or not to amputate. The nurse asked me to take the hat off, but I refused.

"Don't you know?" the doctor asked the nurse. "These are the boys who got smart and lost their minds."

Somehow in all my furious self-destructiveness, I had never considered the possibility of an injury. I had seen myself going out in a blaze. But to live—crippled! My great adventure had failed. At twenty years old, I had discovered that there was no real adventure in the world.

3

The Pebble in the Shell

lay on the hospital bed, my right leg encased in plaster. The doctors told me I would never walk without a cane. At first I had visitors from my unit. Eventually my buddies stopped coming.

But not before they did two things that were to alter events for me.

The first was to mail a letter to Thile I had never intended mailing. I had picked up a habit: Whenever I came back from a night on the town or a battle that left me feeling especially dirty, I would write to Thile. I would put on paper all the filthy, disgusting things I had seen and done, things I could never share with anyone; then I would burn it.

Before I went into my last battle, I had started such a letter to Thile and had left it unfinished in my barracks bag. After I was hit, a buddy went through my bag for personal items. He looked up Thile's name in my address book and mailed the letter. He thought he had been helpful.

As near as I could recall, it began:

Dearest Thile,

I'm so lonely tonight. I wish you were here. I wish I could look right into your eyes as I say all these things and know that you still liked me or at least didn't condemn me.

You wrote me once that I should pray. Well, I'm not the person you think I am. This war used to bother me. But it doesn't anymore. When I see dead people, I shrug. People we've killed, not just soldiers, but ordinary working men and women and children.

I have no desire for God. I don't want to pray. Instead of going to church I go to the pub and drink. . . .

There was much more and much worse. I lay in agony in that hospital ward. Thile was my best friend—and I had wanted her to be so much more.

I thrashed about on the narrow bed, trying to shut out the picture of Thile reading that letter.

As I flung out my arm, my hand fell on the book.

That was the second thing the boys did for me. They found my mother's Bible in the bottom of the duffel bag. Jan Zwart brought it to me, leaving it rather shyly on the bedside table.

But I didn't pick it up. I doubt if I ever would have, except for the nuns. This hospital was run by Franciscan sisters. I fell in love with every one of them. From dawn until

midnight they were busy in the wards, cleaning bedpans, swabbing wounds, writing letters for us, laughing, singing. I never once heard them complain.

One day I asked a nun how it was that she and the other sisters were always so cheerful.

"Why, Andrew, you know the answer to that—a good Dutch boy like you. It's the love of Christ." Her eyes sparkled. "But you're teasing me, aren't you?" She tapped the well-worn Bible on the bedside table. "You've got the answer right here."

In the years since my mother had given it to me, I never once opened it. I propped the book on my chest and turned to Genesis 1:1.

I read the story of creation and of the entrance of sin into the world. I read on. Days later, I came to the New Testament. Lying there encased in plaster, I read straight through the gospels. Could all this really be true?

While I was reading the gospel of John, I received a letter from Thile. I tore it open.

"Dearest Andy," I read. *"I have a letter from a boy who thinks his heart has turned hard. But his heart is breaking and he has shown a little of that heartbreak to me, and I am proud that he has."* Then followed a study outline of the Bible—the only place, Thile wrote, where heartbreak could be understood in terms of God's love.

Wonderful weeks followed. Thile and I read the Bible together, on opposite sides of the earth. I filled pages with questions, and Thile went to her pastor and her own heart to find answers.

Months passed in the hospital, and my cast came off. I saw the shrunken leg and remembered the joys of running that would never be mine again. I found myself holding on to a hard core of resentment.

I started leaving the hospital every evening to hobble painfully to the nearest pub and drink myself into oblivion. The nuns never spoke about it—not until the day before I was to be shipped home. Sister Patrice pulled a chair up to my bed.

"Andy, I have a story for you. Do you know how natives catch monkeys in the forest?"

My face lit up at the thought of a monkey story. "Tell me."

"The natives know that a monkey will never let go of something he wants. So they take a coconut and make a hole in one end just big enough for a monkey's paw to slip through. Then they drop a pebble into the hole and wait in the bushes with a net.

"Eventually a monkey comes along. He'll pick up that coconut shell and rattle it. He'll peer inside. Then he'll slip his paw into the hole and feel around until he gets hold of that pebble. When he tries to bring it out, he cannot get the paw through the hole without letting go. Andy, that monkey will never let go. It's the easiest thing to catch a fellow who acts like that."

Sister Patrice paused for a moment and looked at me.

"Are you holding on to something that's keeping you from your freedom?"

Then she was gone.

4

One Stormy Night

Andrew!" Geltje ran across the little bridge and threw her arms around me.

Maartje ran to kiss me. Ben was there, and his fiancée. Arie, Geltje's new husband, joined us. My young brother Cornelius could not keep his eyes off my cane. In the midst of hugs and kisses, Papa came shuffling around the house, lame himself now. His eyes were moist. "Andrew boy! Good to have you home!" Papa's voice was as loud as ever.

"When you feel like it, Andrew," Maartje said after the greetings were over, "I'll take you out to Mama's grave."

I said that I would like to go right then. The graveyard was five hundred yards from our house. To go even that distance I took Papa's bicycle, threw my bad leg over the seat and pushed myself along, half riding, half walking.

"It's pretty bad, then?" Maartje asked.

"They don't think I'll walk right again."

The ground had not fully settled on Mama's grave. There were fresh flowers in a vase stuck into the soil.

That night I announced I would try taking a walk. No one offered to go with me; they knew what I wanted to do. I got out the bicycle again and hopped and rolled up the street. The cemetery lay in full moonlight, and it was easy to find the grave. I sat on the ground.

"I'm back, Mama." It seemed natural talking to her. "I read your Bible. Not at first, but I did read it. Mama, what am I going to do now? I can't walk without pain making me stop. There's a rehabilitation center at the hospital, but what can I learn there? I feel useless. And guilty for the life I led."

After half an hour I wheeled myself home.

Geltje was at the kitchen table sewing. "We talked about where you could sleep, Andrew," she said. "Do you think you could make it up the ladder?"

I looked at the hole in the ceiling that led to my old attic room. Then I made an assault on that ladder, one rung at a time, putting my good foot up, hauling the other after it. I turned my head so the others did not see my pain. My bed was waiting for me, clean sheets turned down. I lay for a long time staring at the sloping ceiling.

The next morning, taking my cane, I hobbled out to get reacquainted with the village. For some reason, I headed to the Whetstras'. I found them at home and accepted their invitation to coffee.

We sat around the kitchen table while Mr. Whetstra asked me about Indonesia. "Did you find that adventure you were looking for, Andy?"

I looked down. "Not really."

"Well," he said, "we'll just have to keep praying."

I felt the angry flush climb up my neck. "Sure. When adventure calls, I'll limp right out to meet it."

Immediately I was ashamed. What had made me answer like that? I left, feeling I had spoiled a friendship.

Another person I had been eager to see was my boyhood friend Kees. I found him at home, bent over a pile of books. After an awkward greeting, I picked up one of the books.

"What's this?" I asked.

"I've decided I want to go into the ministry," Kees replied.

I left as soon as I politely could.

The veterans' hospital at Doorn was an enormous complex of treatment centers, dormitories and rehabilitation units. Once I moved in, I saw that its chief quality was boredom. On my first weekend leave I went to see Thile. I told myself she could not be as beautiful as I remembered. I limped through the door of her father's fish shop, and she was. Her eyes were blacker, her skin fairer than anyone else's. Our handshake lingered.

"Welcome home, Andrew."

Thile's father came around the counter and shook my hand. "Tell me all about the Indies!"

As soon as I could, I took Thile away from the fish shop. We spent the rest of the afternoon sitting and talking on the wharf. I told her about my homecoming. I told her about the rehabilitation center. I told her my religious life had come to a standstill.

Thile stared out across the harbor. "And yet," she said gently, "God hasn't come to a standstill." She laughed. "I think God has a plan for you, and you keep dodging away."

She turned her dark eyes on mine. "Maybe He wants to make you into something wonderful!"

My eyes fell. I felt so far away from everyone—even Thile. She didn't know what it was like to bite your lip for fear the pain in your leg would make you cry. I left that afternoon knowing I had said things I didn't mean to and none of the things I did.

Two months later at the hospital, several of us were sitting on our beds, reading and writing letters. The nurse announced a visitor. I heard a low whistle rise to the lips of twenty boys. I glanced up. Standing in the doorway was a striking blonde.

"I won't take much of your time," the girl began. "I just want to ask you all to join us at our tent meeting tonight. There will be refreshments—"

"What kind?" someone shouted.

"The bus will leave here at seven o'clock. I hope you can all come."

The boys burst into applause.

When seven o'clock came, every one of us was waiting in the foyer, clean-scrubbed. We were happy, not only because of the night away but also because someone had found our answer to refreshments. By the time the bus arrived at the tent grounds, the bottle was half empty. We took seats in the rear of the tent and finished it.

A man took the podium and announced that there were two people in the congregation who were bound by powers they could not control. Closing his eyes, he began a long prayer for the health of our immortal souls. We choked back our laughter. When he called us "our brethren over whom foreign spirits have gained influence," we howled with laughter. Seeing that further prayer was impossible, the man told the choir to sing. The song they chose was "Let My People Go."

The congregation joined in on the refrain. "Let my people go. . . ."

The meeting ended. But inside my head the words sang on. "Let them go. . . . Let me go. . . ."

The next day during afternoon rest I reached for the Bible on my nightstand. I had not read it since I had been back. But I started reading, and to my astonishment I understood it. All the passages that had seemed so puzzling now read like a fast-paced action yarn. I read straight through the rest period.

A week later the hospital told me I could go home for long weekends. I read the Bible there, stretched out hours on end on my bed in the attic. Geltje would bring me soup, see if I was all right, then go back downstairs without a word.

Then I, who never went to church, started to attend with such regularity that the whole village noticed it.

What was happening?

In November 1949, I was mustered out of the army. With part of my separation pay I bought a new bicycle and learned to pedal, thrusting with the good leg, coasting with the bad. I still could not take a step without pain, but with wheels it no longer mattered so much. Now I started attending church services in neighboring towns. I found a service somewhere every night. At each one I took notes and then spent the following morning looking up passages in the Bible.

Maartje came up the ladder. "Andrew, can I be frank?"

I sat up. "Of course."

"We're worried about the amount of time you're spending up here alone. Always reading the Bible. Going to church every night. What's happened to you, Andy?"

I smiled. "I wish I knew!"

"Papa's worried. He says it's shell shock." With that she backed swiftly down the ladder.

I thought about what she had said. Was I becoming a religious fanatic? I had heard of people who went around quoting Scriptures at everyone. Was I going to get like that?

Still I kept on biking to churches, listening, absorbing.

I began spending time with Kees and with my old school-teacher Miss Meekle, and with the Whetstras. And every week I bicycled to Gorkum to talk over with Thile the things I was reading and hearing.

Thile was thrilled about what was happening to me. But as I continued my rounds of churches, she became alarmed. "Don't you think you ought to pace yourself? Read some different books. Go to the movies."

I couldn't. Nothing interested me except this incredible voyage of discovery. Then Thile began asking if I had found a job. This was a more serious problem. Until I had a job, I could not suggest to Thile the dream I had had so long for her and me. I set out job hunting in earnest.

Then an event occurred that changed my life far more radically than the bullet had a year before. One stormy night, I was in bed. Sleet blew across the polders as it can only blow in Holland in mid-January. There were voices in that wind. I heard Sister Patrice. *"The monkey will never let go. . . ."* I heard the singing under the big tent. *"Let my people go. . . ."*

What was it I was hanging on to? What was standing between me and freedom?

I lay staring at the ceiling and, very quietly, turned myself over to God—lock, stock and adventure. I said, "Lord, if You will show me the way, I will follow You. Amen."

It was as simple as that.

5

The Step of Yes

In the morning I woke with such joy that I had to tell someone. I decided on the Whetstras and my friend Kees.

The Whetstras understood right away. They used words like "born again," and I understood that the step I had taken was along a well-traveled road. Kees also recognized the experience.

To my surprise, though, Thile did not seem as pleased. Wasn't this the thing people did at mass rallies? she asked.

A few weeks later I went to Amsterdam with Kees to hear an evangelist, Arne Donker. Toward the end of his sermon, Pastor Donker said, "I've had the feeling all night that someone in the audience wants to give himself to the mission field." He peered out over the audience.

The silence in the hall grew. "Let's get out of here!" Kees whispered.

We edged our way to the end of our row. Heads turned eagerly. We both sat down.

"Well," said Mr. Donker at last, "God knows who it is."

People looked around as if to spot whom the preacher meant. Then, in obedience to some summons I shall never understand, both Kees and I were on our feet.

"Ah, yes," the preacher said. "There you are. Will you boys come forward?"

With a sigh, we walked down the long aisle to the front of the meeting hall, where we knelt to hear Mr. Donker say a prayer over us. All I could think of was what Thile would say.

After he finished praying, the preacher told Kees and me that he wanted to see us after the service. Reluctantly, and half suspecting him of being a hypnotist, we stayed behind. When the hall was empty, Mr. Donker asked us our names.

"Andrew and Kees," he repeated. "Where do you come from, boys?"

"Witte."

"Excellent! Here's your first assignment. I want you to hold an open-air meeting in front of the burgomaster's house in Witte. Jesus told the disciples to spread the Good News starting in their own backyard. . . ."

The words exploded in my mind.

"I'll be with you, boys!" Mr. Donker went on. "Nothing to be alarmed about. I'll speak first. . . ."

I was barely listening. I was remembering how much I disliked street preachers.

". . . So we have a date. Saturday afternoon in Witte."

"Yes, sir," we said, intending to say no.

Kees and I rode the bus home in stunned silence.

Not a soul in Witte missed that meeting. Even the town dogs turned out for the show. We stood with the evangelist on a little platform and looked out over a sea of familiar faces. Some were laughing, some only grinning. The Whetstras and Miss Meekle nodded encouragement.

It was a nightmare. I don't remember a thing Kees and Mr. Donker said. I only remember the moment Mr. Donker turned toward me and waited. I could not remember a thing I had planned to say. All I could do was tell how I felt guilty coming home from Indonesia. How I had carried around the burden of what I was, until one night I laid it down. I told them how free I had felt ever since—that is, until Mr. Donker here trapped me into saying I wanted to become a missionary.

"But you know," I said to my hometown, "I might surprise him. . . ."

I dreaded my next date with Thile. It is hard to tell the girl you hope to marry that you have decided to be a missionary. What kind of life was that? Hard work, little pay, disagreeable living conditions in some far-off place. How could I suggest such a life to her, unless she herself were heart and soul committed to the idea?

I started my campaign to make a missionary out of Thile. I told her about the moment when the conviction had hit me and how sure I had been since of God's hand in this.

"One thing I agree with Mr. Donker," she said. "The place to start any ministry is at home. Why don't you get a job around Witte and consider that your mission field first?"

This made sense.

The largest industry anywhere near Witte was the huge Ringers' chocolate factory in Alkmaar. Soon I was at their hiring office.

"Next!"

I walked in as briskly as I could. Walking was still painful, but I had learned to step on the injured ankle without limping. The personnel director scowled at my application form.

"Medical discharge," he read aloud. "What's the matter with you?"

"Nothing," I said. "I can do anything anyone here can do."

He gave me a job. I was to count the boxes at the end of one of the packaging assemblies, then wheel them to the shipping room. A boy led me through a maze of corridors and pushed open the door to an enormous assembly room where perhaps two hundred girls worked around a dozen conveyer belts.

"Girls, this is Andrew."

To my astonishment, a chorus of whistles greeted this introduction. Then, shouted suggestions.

"Hey, Ruthie, how would you like him?"

"Can't tell by looking."

The leader of the wisecracking, I noted, was a girl named Greetje. I was grateful when I could escape to the shipping room.

Too soon, I had to run the gamut of whistles in the big room again. *This may be a mission field,* I thought, *but I'll never learn to talk to these girls.*

I stopped. Smiling at me through the glass partition of the timekeeper's booth were the warmest eyes I had ever seen. They were brown. No, they were green. She was blond, slender and young, and she handled the work orders and finished-work receipts. As I handed mine through the window, her smile broke into a laugh.

"Don't mind them," she said gently. "They treat every newcomer this way."

She handed me a new shipping order, but still I stood there, staring at her eyes. They were never the same shade twice. I felt sure I had seen her before.

The hours dragged. By the end of the long day on my feet, every step on my ankle was agony. I began to limp. Greetje spotted it at once.

"What's the matter, Andy?" she shrieked. "Fall out of bed?"

"East Indies," I said, hoping to shut her up.

Greetje's yelp of triumph could be heard all over the room. "We got a war hero, girls!" For days the girls questioned me about what they imagined to be the exotic life of the East.

I might have quit except for the smiling eyes behind the glass partition. I went there even when I had no receipt to deliver. I wondered how she felt about the talk she overheard.

It was a month before I got up the courage to say, "I'm worried about you. You're too young to be working with this crowd."

The girl threw back her head and laughed. "Why, Grampa! What old-fashioned ideas you have! Actually"—she leaned close to the window—"they're not a bad crowd. Most of them need friends, and they don't know any other way to get them."

She considered me as though wondering whether to confide in me. "You see," she said softly, "I'm a Christian. That's why I came to work here."

I gaped in astonishment at my fellow missionary. Then I remembered where I had seen her before. The veterans' hospital! This was the girl who had invited us to the tent meeting!

I stumbled over my words, telling her how I had come here on the same mission as her own. Her name was Corry van Dam, and from that day on she and I were a team. My job took me up and down the rows of packagers. I could keep a lookout for anyone with problems. I would pass the word to Corry, who could speak to the girl in private.

We eventually found other people interested in the same things we were. The British evangelist Sidney Wilson was holding "youth weekends" in the Netherlands, and we started attending these.

One of the first people to come with us was Amy, a blind girl who worked on the same belt with Greetje, who teased her unmercifully. Usually Amy took it in good humor. But one day I found her blinking back tears.

Greetje grinned maliciously. "All men are alike in the dark, eh, Amy?" she shouted.

I stopped in the doorway. I had prayed that morning, as I always did, that God would tell me what to say to people.

The order I seemed to be getting now was so unexpected I could hardly believe it, but so clear that I obeyed without thinking.

"Greetje," I called across the room, "shut up!"

Her jaw literally dropped. I was startled myself.

"Greetje," I shouted again, "the bus leaves for the conference center at nine Saturday morning. I want you on board."

"All right."

Her answer came that quickly. The entire room was silent.

On Saturday, Greetje was aboard the bus. She was her old self, though, saying she was there only to find out what really went on after the lights went off. During the meetings she made quiet comments while people told how God was making a difference in their lives. Between meetings she read a romance magazine.

The bus brought us back to Alkmaar, where I had left my bicycle at the depot. Greetje lived near Witte. I wondered if she would ride with me on the back of my bike.

"Can I give you a lift home, Greetje? Save you the bus fare?"

I could tell she was weighing riding with me against the price of the bus ticket. Finally, she shrugged and climbed onto the seat at the rear of my bike.

As soon as we were out in the country, I intended to face Greetje with her need for God. But to my astonishment, the clear command that came this time was *Not one word about religion. Just admire the scenery.*

I could scarcely believe I heard correctly. But I obeyed. During the entire trip I did not say a word to my captive about religion. Instead, I talked about the tulip fields we passed and discovered she, too, had eaten tulip bulbs during the war. When we got to her street, she actually smiled.

Next day at the factory, Greetje didn't crack one dirty joke. When Amy dropped a box of chocolates, Greetje knelt down and retrieved the pieces.

At lunchtime she plunked her tray down beside mine. "Can I sit with you?"

"Of course."

Greetje began. "I thought you would high-pressure me into 'making a decision for Christ,' like they said at those meetings. Then you didn't say a word. I began to wonder, 'Does Andrew think I've gone so far there's no turning back? Is that why he doesn't bother?' Then I began to wonder if God would still listen if I said I was sorry. Would He let me start over, like those kids claimed? Anyhow, I asked Him to. And, Andy, I cried almost all night. But this morning I feel great."

Overnight Greetje was a changed person. She was still a leader, she still talked all the time—but what a difference. When Greetje stopped telling smutty stories, the other girls stopped, too.

A prayer cell started in the factory, with Greetje in charge of attendance. If someone's child was sick, if a husband was out of work, Greetje found out about it, and woe to the worker who didn't put some money in the hat. The change in this girl was complete and it was permanent. Night after night, I went to sleep thanking God for letting me have a part in this transformation. That factory was a different place.

One day when I pedaled through the main gate, I had a surprise waiting for me.

"Mr. Ringers wants to see you," Corry said.

A secretary held open the door to the president's office. Mr. Ringers sat in an enormous armchair and waved me into another.

"Andrew," said Mr. Ringers, "do you remember the psychological tests we finished about two weeks ago?"

"Yes, sir."

"They show that you have an exceptional I.Q."

I didn't know what an "I.Q." was, but since he was smiling, I smiled, too.

"We have decided," he went on, "to put you in our management training course. I want you to take two weeks to walk through the factory and examine every job. When you find one you like, we'll train you for it."

Finally I found my voice. "I know the job I'd like. I'd like to be that man who talked to me after I finished the tests."

"A job analyst," said Mr. Ringers. His eyes bored into mine. "I suppose that while discussing jobs, you wouldn't object if the subject of religion came up?"

I felt my face turning scarlet.

"We know what you've been doing," he said. "I consider your kind of work considerably more important than manufacturing chocolates." He smiled. "I don't know any reason, Andrew, why you can't do both. If you can help me to run a better factory while getting recruits for God's Kingdom, I'll be satisfied."

Thile was ecstatic at my new job. She hoped I would find it so interesting that I would forget the missionary idea. But although I loved the new work, I felt more persuaded that I was called to something else. In return for my training I agreed to stay at Ringers' two years. When that time was up, I knew I would leave.

Thile stopped arguing and pitched in to help. Her own church was the Dutch Reformed, which had many overseas missions. She wrote to them, asking about qualifications for serving. All gave the same answer: Ordination was the first step.

Making up the schooling I missed during the war and then studying theology would take twelve years! My heart sank. Nevertheless, I enrolled in some correspondence courses and began to grow a library—a German grammar, an English grammar, a volume of church history, a Bible commentary. For two years I spent every spare moment reading.

When Miss Meekle learned what I was doing, she offered to coach me in English. She was a wonderful teacher. If her pronunciation seemed different from the English I heard on the radio, I put it down to faulty electronics.

Miss Meekle wondered about seminary. "Do you really need to be ordained to help people?" she asked. "Surely there's useful work for laymen in the missions?"

It was the question I asked myself. I discussed it with Sidney Wilson. I grumbled about the delays, and he began to laugh.

"You talk like the people at WEC," he said. "Worldwide Evangelization Crusade, an English group that trains missionaries to go to parts of the world where churches don't have programs. They feel like you about waiting."

If WEC thought God wanted a man in a certain place, he explained, they sent him there and trusted God to handle the details. "If they think a man has a genuine call and commitment, they don't care about a degree. They train him for two years and send him out."

Kees, who had been studying for ordination, was most interested when I told him what Mr. Wilson said. "Theologically that's sound," Kees said. "I'd like to know more about WEC."

A few months later Sidney Wilson told me a man from WEC headquarters was visiting Haarlem, so I biked there to meet him. When this man talked about the work the mission was doing all over the world, his face came alive. He gave the credit to the WEC training school in Glasgow, Scotland, and to its teachers, who mostly served without pay. They included doctors of theology and other subjects but also bricklayers and plumbers and electricians. Students were trained to start missions where none existed. But the true aim of the school was to turn out the best Christians these students were capable of being.

I saw Kees as soon as I got back to Witte. He had many questions: How much were the fees? When did the next session begin? What were the language requirements? Soon Kees applied for admission to the Glasgow school and was accepted.

I received letters from Kees, describing his life there, his courses, his discoveries in Christian living. I had been at the factory longer than the two years I promised Mr.

Ringers. Surely this WEC school was the right place for me, too.

Still, I didn't have Kees's education. And hide it though I might from others, I had a crippled ankle. How could I be a missionary if I could not walk without pain!

I had heard Sidney Wilson speak of "praying through," which meant sticking with a prayer until he got an answer. I decided to try it. One Sunday afternoon I went out to the polders. I sat on the edge of a canal and began talking to God. I prayed right through Sunday afternoon and into the evening.

"What is it, Lord? What am I holding back? What am I using as an excuse for not serving You?"

I finally had my answer, there by the canal. My "yes" to God had always been a "yes, but." Yes, but I'm not educated. Yes, but I'm lame.

Now with the next breath, I said yes in a brand-new way. "Whenever, wherever, however You want me, I'll go. I'll begin this very minute. Lord, as I stand and take my first step forward, I'll call it the Step of Yes."

I stood and took a step. I felt a sharp wrench in the lame leg. I thought I had turned my crippled ankle. Gingerly I put the foot on the ground. I could stand on it all right, and cautiously I walked home. A verse of Scripture popped into my mind: "Going, they were healed."

Was it possible I, too, had been healed?

I was due at a Sunday evening service in a village six kilometers away. I decided to *walk* to the meeting.

And I did.

My family could not believe it. They had seen my bicycle and assumed I had changed my mind.

The next day my ankle began to itch. I rubbed the old scar, and two stitches came through the skin. A few days later, the incision, which had never healed properly, closed.

The following week I applied for admission to the WEC Missionary Training College in Glasgow. A month later the reply came. Dependent on space opening up in the men's dormitory, I could start in May.

Corry had news, too. She was leaving Ringers' to begin nurse's training. I looked into her sparkling eyes and decided finally that they were hazel. We held hands a moment, then quickly said good-bye.

I dreaded telling Thile that I had enrolled in a school sponsored by no church and supported by no organization. We spent a miserable afternoon walking along the waterfront. Instead of arguing, Thile grew silent. But when I mentioned the healing of my leg and called it a miracle, she flared up. "Injuries improve every day. Most people don't go around making wild claims."

I didn't stay for dinner with Thile's folks that night. Thile needed time to get used to the new plans.

I set about raising money for my trip. I sold my bicycle and my books and purchased a ticket to London, where I was to meet the directors of the WEC before heading for Glasgow.

But before I left for London, three things happened that left me reeling.

The first was a letter from Thile. She had written to the board of missions of her church, asking their opinion of the school in Glasgow. They had replied that it had no standing in any mission circle with which they were involved.

This being the case, Thile went on, she would prefer neither to see nor to hear from me as long as I was associated with this group.

As I stood in the doorway holding the letter, Miss Meekle crossed the bridge to our house.

"Andrew," she said, "there's something I want to tell you." She took a deep breath. "I've never actually *heard* any English. But I've read a lot of it," she added, "and a lady I write to in England says my grammar is perfect." She paused. "I just thought I'd tell you." And she fled.

Two days later, a telegram arrived from London: "Regret to inform you expected vacancy has not materialized. Request for admission denied. You may re-apply 1954."

Three blows in a row. There was no room for me in the school. I probably could not speak the language in which the courses were taught. And if I went, I would lose my girl.

But inside me a voice seemed to say, *Go*. It was the voice that had called to me in the wind, the voice that had told me to speak out in the factory, the voice that never made sense at a logical level.

The next day I kissed my family good-bye and started on my journey.

6

The Royal Way

I stepped off the train in London and made my way to the address of the Worldwide Evangelization Crusade headquarters—a large building in need of paint.

A woman answered the door and gestured for me to come in, then found a man who spoke some Dutch. I explained who I was.

"Didn't you get our cable? We wired you three days ago that there was no room in Glasgow just now."

"I got the cable, yes."

"And you came anyhow?" The man smiled.

"A place will open for me when the time comes," I said. "I want to be ready."

The man smiled again. He talked with his colleagues, then said it would be all right for me to stay for a while, provided I was willing to work.

So began the hardest two months of my life.

The physical work was not difficult: I was to paint the WEC headquarters building, and I enjoyed the job. What was difficult was learning English. I worked so hard on the language that my head ached.

At WEC they practiced Morning Quiet Time, where they got up before breakfast to read their Bibles and pray. I liked the idea and was up with the birds, dressed and in the garden with an English Bible and a dictionary. This technique had some disadvantages. My English was filled with *thees* and *thous*. One time I passed on a request for butter by saying, "Thus sayeth the neighbor of Andrew, that thou wouldst be pleased to pass the butter."

But I was learning. Eventually the director asked me to lead the evening devotional. After seven minutes I ran out of English words and sat down. Two weeks later I was asked to speak again. This time I spoke for fourteen minutes.

My new friends gathered around. "You're getting better, Andy," they said, pounding me on the back. "We could almost understand you!"

"So this is our Dutchman. . . . I think his sermon was very fine indeed."

The voice came from the back of the room and belonged to a middle-aged man I had not seen before. I was struck by the sparkle in his eyes.

"Andrew, this is William Hopkins," the WEC director said.

William Hopkins took my hand in both of his own large hands. "He looks strong enough," he said. "I think he will do very well."

The director explained that the time had come for me to leave the headquarters building. My bed was needed for a returning missionary. But if Mr. Hopkins could get me British working papers, I could get a job in London and start saving money for Glasgow.

"Go get your things, Andrew m'boy," Mr. Hopkins said. "You're coming to live with Mrs. Hopkins and meself."

While I packed, one of the WEC workers told me about Mr. Hopkins. He was a successful contractor who gave away nine-tenths of his income to various missions, including WEC.

The Hopkinses' living quarters on the Thames River were simple and homey. Mrs. Hopkins was an invalid who spent most days in bed.

"You make yourself to home here," she greeted me. "You'll find the cupboard, and you'll learn that the front door is never latched." Her eyes sparkled like her husband's. "And don't be surprised should you find a stray in your bed some night. If that happens, there's blankets and pillows in the living room, and you can make a bedroll."

Within the week, one evening when I came back to the house, I found Mr. and Mrs. Hopkins in the living room.

"Don't go to your room, Andrew," Mrs. Hopkins said. "There's a drunk in your bed."

As I ate supper in front of the fire, she told me Mr. Hopkins had brought the man home. "When he wakes up, we'll find him some food and some clothes," Mrs. Hopkins said. "God will supply."

And God did. On dozens of occasions while I stayed with the Hopkinses, I saw God meet their practical needs in the most unusual ways. Never once did I see anyone go hungry or coatless from their house. The profits of Mr. Hopkins's business supplied their own modest needs. Strangers such as myself and the beggars and drunks who passed through their doors had to be fed by God.

Perhaps a neighbor dropped by with a casserole. "Just in case you're not feeling up to cooking tonight, ducky." Or one of the previous bed-tenants returned to see if he could help. "Yes, you can. We have a man in the bed tonight who has no shoes. Could you find him a pair?"

I intended to stay with the Hopkinses until I got working papers and found a job. But though I went to the labor ministry again and again, the work permit was never granted.

Then I was invited by the Hopkinses to stay on in their home. The first morning after I arrived, Mr. Hopkins went to work, Mrs. Hopkins had to stay in bed, and I was left to myself. I found a mop and scrubbed the kitchen floor and the bathroom. I found the dirty clothes bin, so I washed clothes. When they were dry, I ironed them. Then I cooked dinner.

I was used to doing these things at home. But the Hopkinses were thunderstruck. They felt I had done something remarkable and asked me to stay on as family.

So I did. I became chief cook and bottle washer, and they became my English mother and father. I called them Uncle Hoppy and Mother Hoppy. In many ways Mrs. Hopkins reminded me of my mother, both in her uncomplaining ways and in the open door to the needy.

Uncle Hoppy had a storefront mission. Its doors were always open, and occasionally a stray derelict would wander in for some warmth. But when it came time for services, I remember one day hearing him preach an entire sermon to empty chairs.

When the sermon ended, I objected. "When I preach someday, I want to see real people."

Uncle Hoppy only laughed. "Just you wait," he said. "Before we get home, we will meet the man who was supposed to be here. When we do, his heart will be prepared."

Sure enough, as we were walking home, we were approached by a street person, and Uncle Hoppy plunged into the conclusion of his sermon. That night I slept in the living room again, and by morning the street person was a new Christian.

At last one day came a letter from Glasgow: I was to report for the fall term.

We did a triumphal march around Mother Hoppy's bed— Uncle Hoppy, a stray vagabond and I—until we realized it meant saying good-bye.

I left London in September 1953 for the missionary training school in Scotland. When I arrived at the address I had been given, I found a tall two-story house on the corner. Over the entrance were the words "Have Faith In God."

Kees answered the door. How good it was to look into that solid Dutch face again. After we slapped one another's shoulders many times, he seized my bag and ushered me to my top-floor room. He introduced me to my three roommates and pointed out where the rest of the 45 young people slept—men in one of the attached houses, women in the other.

Kees sat with me through the introduction to the director, Steward Dinnen. "The real purpose of this training," Mr. Dinnen said, "is to teach our students they can trust God to do what He has said He would do. We don't go into traditional missionary fields, but into new territory. Our graduates are on their own. They cannot be effective if they are afraid or if they doubt that God really means what He says in His Word. I hope this is what you are looking for, Andrew."

"Yes, sir. Exactly."

"You know that we charge no tuition. The teachers, the London people, myself—none of us receives a salary. Room and board and other physical costs for the year come to ninety pounds—a little over two hundred and fifty dollars. Students do the cooking and cleaning. You can pay in installments, thirty pounds at the start of each session. But we like the installments paid on time."

This was going to be my first experiment in trusting God for material needs. I had thirty pounds for the first semester's fee. After that I looked forward to seeing how God would supply the money.

During the first few weeks, something bothered me. At mealtimes the students would frequently discuss inadequate funds. Sometimes after a whole night in prayer for a certain need, half of the request would be granted, or three-quarters. For example, if an old people's home where students conducted services needed ten blankets, the students would receive enough to buy six. The Bible said we worked in God's vineyard. Was this the way the Lord of the vineyard paid His hired men?

One night I went for a long walk. Students had warned me not to go into Patrick, the slum at the bottom of our hill. It was home to addicts, drunks, thieves, even murderers. And yet this area drew me now as if it had something to say.

Within five blocks of walking in the dirty gray streets of Patrick, I was accosted twice by beggars. I gave them all the money I had. Beggars in the streets of the Glasgow slums would have a better income than the missionaries-in-training up the hill. I could not understand why this bothered me.

Walking back up the hill toward the school, I had my answer. It was not about money. It was about a relationship.

At the chocolate factory I had trusted Mr. Ringers to pay me in full and on time. If an ordinary factory worker could be financially secure, so could one of God's workers.

I walked up the front steps, certain that I was on the verge of something exciting. The school was asleep. I tiptoed upstairs and sat by the window, looking out over Glasgow. If I were going to give my life as a servant of the King, I had to know that King. In what *way* could I trust Him? Because if He were a King in name only, I would go back to the chocolate factory.

But suppose I discovered God to be a Person, in the sense that He communicated and cared and loved. That was the kind of King I would follow into battle.

That night, I knew that my probing into God's nature would begin with this issue of money. I knelt in front of the window and made a covenant with Him. "Lord," I said, "I need to know if I can trust You in practical things. I thank You for letting me earn the fees for the first semester. I ask

You now to supply the rest. If I have to be even a day late in paying, I'll know I'm to go back to the chocolate factory."

God honored my prayer. But not without first testing me in some amusing ways.

The first semester sped by. Mornings we spent in classrooms studying courses taught in any seminary. In the afternoon we learned bricklaying, plumbing, carpentry, first aid, tropical hygiene, motor repair. For several weeks all of us, girls as well as boys, worked at the Ford factory in London, learning how to take a car apart and put it together. Besides these standard trades, we learned how to build huts out of palm fronds and how to make mud jars that would hold water. We took turns in the kitchen and the laundry and the garden. No one was exempt.

Soon came time to head out on the first of several training trips in evangelism. "You're going to like this, Andy," said Mr. Dinnen. "It's an exercise in trust. The rules are simple. Each student on your team is given a one-pound banknote. With that you go on a missionary tour through Scotland. You're expected to pay your own transportation, your own lodging, your food, renting of halls, providing refreshments—"

"All on a one-pound note?"

"Worse than that. When you get back to school after four weeks, you're expected to pay back the pound!"

I laughed. "Sounds like we'll be passing the hat all the time."

"No, you're not allowed to mention money at your meetings. All your needs must be provided without any manipulation on your part—or the experiment is a failure."

I was a member of a team of five boys. Later when I tried to remember where our funds came from during those four weeks, it was hard to. What we needed was always there. Sometimes someone's parents would send a little money. Sometimes we would get a check in the mail from a church we had visited earlier. The notes that came with these gifts were always interesting. "I know you don't need money or you would have mentioned it," someone would write. "But God wouldn't let me sleep tonight until I had put this in an envelope for you."

Contributions frequently came in the form of produce. In a town in the highlands, we were given six hundred eggs. We had eggs for breakfast, eggs for lunch, eggs as hors d'oeuvres before a dinner of eggs with an egg-white meringue dessert. It was weeks before we could look a chicken in the eye.

But money or produce, we stuck fast to two rules: We never mentioned a need, and we gave away a tithe—one-tenth—of whatever came to us, within 24 hours if possible.

Another team also set aside ten percent, but they didn't give it away immediately, "in case of an emergency." They ended up owing money to hotels, lecture halls and markets all over Scotland. We came back to school almost ten pounds ahead. As fast as we gave money away, God was swifter.

So I was not really surprised when we got back to school to find a check from the Whetstras for exactly enough to pay my second term's fee.

The second term seemed to go even faster than the first. Before that term was over, I had received money to keep me there a third, this time from buddies at the veterans' hospital.

I never mentioned school fees to anyone, and yet the gifts always came so that I could pay them on time. They never contained more than the school costs, and they never came two together.

God's faithfulness I experienced continually. Should a need arise, God would supply it.

And a true need did arise.

Foreigners in Britain renewed their visas at periodic intervals. Mine had to be renewed by December 31, 1954, or I would have to leave the country. But when December rolled around, I did not have a cent. How was I going to get the forms to London? A registered letter cost one shilling—twelve pennies. I did not believe that God was going to let me be thrown out of school for lack of a shilling.

So the game moved into a new phase. I called it the Game of the Royal Way, because when God supplied money, He did it in a kingly manner, not in some groveling way.

Three separate times, over the matter of that registered letter, I was almost lured from the Royal Way. I was, that last year, head of the student body and in charge of the school's tract fund. One day my eye lit first on the calendar—December 28—and then on the fund, which contained several pounds. Surely it would be all right to borrow just one shilling.

Quickly I put the idea behind me.

Then it was December 29. Two days left. It occurred to me I might *find* those pennies lying on the ground.

I had put on my coat and started down the street before I saw what I was doing—walking along with head bowed, eyes on the ground, searching the gutter for pennies. What kind of Royal Way was this! I laughed out loud there on the busy street. Then I walked back to school with my head high.

December 30 arrived. I had to have my application in the mail that day.

Midmorning, someone shouted upstairs that I had a visitor. This must be my delivering angel! But when I saw who it was, my heart dropped. Richard, a friend I had made in the Patrick slums, came to me when he needed money.

I went outside to where Richard stood, hands in pockets, eyes lowered. "Andrew," he said, "would you have a little extra cash?"

As I was about to explain why I had no cash, I saw the coin.

A shilling lay among the pebbles, the sun glinting off it in such a way that I could see it but not Richard. I stuck out my foot and covered the coin. As we talked, I picked up the coin with a handful of pebbles. I tossed the pebbles down, aimlessly, until I had just the shilling in my hand. That coin meant I could stay in school. I would not be doing Richard a favor by giving it to him—he would probably spend it on drink.

While I thought up arguments, I knew it was no good. How could I judge Richard when Christ told me so clearly that I must not? Furthermore, this was not the Royal Way! What right had I to hold on to money? I held out the coin.

"Look, Richard," I said. "Would it help?"

Richard's eyes lit up. "It would, mate."

With a light heart, I turned to go inside.

Before I reached the door the postman turned down our walk. In the mail was a letter for me. I knew when I saw the handwriting that it was from the prayer group at Ringers' and that there would be cash inside. There was. A lot of cash. More than enough to send my letter.

The King had done it His way.

In spring 1955, my two years at the Missionary Training College were almost over. Kees had graduated the year before and was in Korea. The director asked me if I would consider joining him.

But one morning, without fanfare, I picked up a magazine, and my life has never been the same since.

The week before graduation I went into the basement to get my suitcase. On top of a cardboard box was a magazine that neither I nor anyone else at the school remembered seeing before.

I picked it up. It was a beautiful magazine, printed on glossy paper, with color pictures showing marching youths parading the streets of Peking and Warsaw and Prague. Their faces were animated. The text told me these young people were part of a worldwide organization 96 million strong. They were Communists, and yet nowhere was the word Communist used. The talk was all of a better world, a bright tomorrow.

Then I saw the announcement of a youth festival to be held in Warsaw in July. Everyone was invited.

I took the magazine to my room. That night, with no idea where it would lead, I wrote to the Warsaw address mentioned in the magazine. I told them frankly that I was training to be a Christian missionary, and that I was interested in going to the youth festival to exchange ideas: I would talk about Christ, they could talk about socialism. Would they allow me to come under these circumstances?

I posted the letter, and back bounced an answer. Most certainly they wanted me to come. As a student, my rate was reduced. A special train would leave from Amsterdam. They looked forward to seeing me in Warsaw.

The only person I told about this trip was Uncle Hoppy, who wrote back, "Andrew, I think you should go. I am enclosing fifty pounds for your expenses."

As I left Scotland to go home to Holland, a dream began to take shape.

7

Behind the Iron Curtain

My family was overjoyed to see me come home. There were the shouts and hugs and catching up.

For several days I visited friends. I saw Mr. Ringers at the factory. I visited Miss Meekle, who was astonished by my English. I called on the Whetstras and learned they were moving to Amsterdam.

I visited my brother Ben and his wife. I asked if he had heard anything about Thile. He said he read she had married a baker.

Amsterdam, July 15, 1955. Hundreds of young men and women milled about the train station to go to the festival in Warsaw.

My suitcase contained a few clothes and lots of small booklets titled "The Way of Salvation" and translated into every European language.

A few hours later I stood in Warsaw's Central Station, waiting for my hotel assignment. I knew not a single person in Poland. Thousands of young people were converging on Warsaw for purposes opposite my own.

My "hotel" turned out to be a school that had been converted into a dormitory for this occasion. I was assigned to a mathematics classroom that held thirty beds. As soon as possible I left the hotel and went into the Warsaw streets, wondering what to do. I boarded a bus, and as we wove our way through traffic, I knew what I was supposed to do.

I had learned a little German during the occupation, and I knew that there was a large German-speaking minority in Poland. Taking a deep breath, I said in German, "I am a Christian from Holland." Everyone stopped talking. "I want to meet some Polish Christians. Can anyone help me?"

Silence. But as a woman rose to leave the bus, she pressed her face near mine and whispered an address and the words "Bible shop."

A Bible shop in a Communist country?

I found the address, and it was a Bible shop plain as day. The window was filled with Bibles, red-letter editions, foreign translations, pocket Testaments. But the door was padlocked. There was a notice on the door, which I copied word for word and took back to the hotel.

"It's a notice of vacation," my group leader said. "'Closed for holidays. Will open again July 21.'"

So I had to wait.

Our routine for three weeks was established. Go on official sightseeing tours in the morning and listen to speeches in the afternoon and evening.

I followed the routine for a few days. We were shown a well-scrubbed face of Warsaw. New schools, thriving factories, high-rise apartments, overflowing shops. It was impressive. But I wondered what I would see if I managed to get off by myself. So one morning before the rest of my group came down for breakfast, I was out of the building.

Up and down the avenues of Warsaw I walked, saddened by the signs of war violence. Whole blocks were bombed out, blocks the sightseeing tours had avoided. There were slums, food shops with long lines, men and women wearing rags for clothes. In a bombed-out section of town, families had dug their way into the basements and were making their homes in the rubble.

Sunday came. We were to take part in a demonstration. Instead, I went to church.

Newspapers back home had given me the impression that religion in Poland had gone underground. This was not so. The Bible shop was apparently still operating. I passed Catholic churches with the doors wide open. Eventually I found myself seated at a Reformed church service behind the Iron Curtain—that invisible divider between the free world and those nations under Communist rule.

I was surprised that the church was about three-quarters full with many young people. The singing was enthusiastic. During his sermon, the preacher constantly referred to his Bible. When the service was over, I waited in the back

of the sanctuary to see if I could find anyone who spoke a language I spoke. Before long I heard, "Welcome."

I turned and found myself looking at the pastor. "Could you wait a moment?" he said in English. "I should like to speak with you."

After most of the congregation left, the pastor and a handful of young people volunteered to answer my questions. Yes, they worshiped openly and with considerable freedom, as long as they stayed clear of political subjects. There were members of the church who were also members of the Communist Party. The regime had done so much for the people that one just closed an eye to the rest.

"What church do you belong to at home?" one youth asked.

"Baptist."

"Would you like to go to a Baptist service? There's one tonight." He wrote down an address.

That evening the service was already in progress when I arrived. This was a smaller turnout, with few teenagers. But an interesting thing happened. Word passed to the minister that a foreigner was in the congregation. I was asked to come up on the platform and speak. Did they have this much freedom?

"Does anyone here speak German or English?" I asked. A woman in the congregation spoke German, and through her I preached my first sermon behind the Iron Curtain.

At the end the pastor said, "We want to thank you for *being* here. Even if you had not said a word, seeing you means so much. We feel at times that we are all alone in our struggle."

That night, I thought about how different these two churches had been. One cooperated with the government: It attracted larger crowds, and it was acceptable to young people.

The other walked a lonelier path. When I asked if Party members attended their services, the answer was "Not that we *know* about!"

I was learning so much.

At last came the day the Bible shop reopened. I left the hotel early and walked to the address. Just before nine o'clock a man hurried down the street, stopped in front of the Bible shop and unlocked the door.

"Good morning," I said in Polish.

The man looked at me. "Good morning," he said a trifle distantly.

"Do you speak either English or German?" I asked in English.

"English." He looked up the street. "Come in."

The proprietor switched on lights and began raising shades. While he worked, I introduced myself. The proprietor showed me his shop: his many editions of the Bible, the wide range of prices available. All the while he questioned me, trying to establish who I really was.

"Why are you in Poland?" he asked suddenly.

"If one member suffers, all suffer together," I quoted from 1 Corinthians.

The proprietor looked at me. "We have not been talking about suffering," he said. "On the contrary, I have been telling you how free we are to publish and distribute Bibles."

I asked if there were Bible stores in other Communist countries. "Some yes, some no," he said. "I understand that in Russia Bibles are very scarce. They tell me fortunes are being made there. A man smuggles ten Bibles into Russia and sells them for enough to buy a motorcycle. He drives the motorcycle back into Poland or Yugoslavia or East Germany and sells it for a fat profit, with which he buys more Bibles."

All morning I visited with the Bible shop owner. When I walked back to the school, I tried to make sense of the visit. Here was a store selling Bibles openly to anyone who wanted one—hardly an example of the religious persecution we had so often heard about in the Netherlands. And yet my friend was as cautious and tense as if he were carrying on an illegal trade. All was not as it seemed.

I wanted to hand out my booklets on the street, to see what would happen. So for several days I stood on corners, went to the marketplace, rode the trams, and everywhere I handed out my booklets.

I had never seen trams as crowded as these. Once as I squeezed onto a crowded platform, I held my tracts over my head so they would not be crushed. A woman near me looked up at the pamphlets and crossed herself.

"*Ja*," she said in German. "This is what we need in Poland."

The Catholic from Eastern Europe and the Protestant from the West, there on the crowded tramway platform, met as Christians.

The days passed. No evil consequences followed the distribution of my booklets. I began to feel exhilarated about this mission field.

I thought about the military barracks up the street from the school. It had not occurred to me to pass out booklets to the soldiers there. The sight of their uniforms made me hurry in the other direction.

I of all people should have known the uniform doesn't make the man. The day before the festival ended, I walked up to the group of six soldiers standing guard and handed each of them a booklet. The men glanced at the booklets, at me, and then at each other.

Suddenly they came to attention. Up walked an officer, barking orders in Polish. The six soldiers wheeled smartly and marched away. I noticed they carried their booklets with them.

"What did you give these men?" said the officer in German.

"This, sir." I handed him a booklet. He looked at it carefully. Two hours later it was I who broke away, and as we parted, the officer, a Russian Orthodox by birth, wished me Godspeed.

The next morning was our last in Warsaw. I was on the street at sunup. I found a bench on one of the avenues and sat down with my pocket Testament on my knee. I wanted to pray for each person I had encountered on my trip. I pictured the places and the people I had seen. On three Sundays I visited Presbyterian, Baptist, Roman Catholic, Orthodox, Reformed and Methodist churches. Five times I was asked to speak during a service. I visited a Bible shop, talked with a military officer, and talked with people on street corners and on trolley cars. I prayed for each one.

As I prayed, I heard the music.

It was coming toward me down the avenue. It sounded martial and smart, with voices singing. It was the Parade of Triumph that ended the festival.

This was the other side of the picture. Against one Bible shop and the occasional Christian I met was the regime.

Here they came, young Socialists, marching down the avenue. They marched because they believed. They marched singing, their voices like shouts. On they came for fifteen minutes, rank after rank of young men and young women. . . .

The effect was overwhelming. These people were shouting their good news. And part of the news was that superstitions of religion no longer held. Man was his own master.

What should we do about these thousands of young people marching, clapping with a terrifying rhythm?

What should *I* do?

The Bible in my lap lay open to the book of Revelation. My fingers rested on the page almost as though they were pointing. "Awake," said the verse at my fingertips, "and strengthen what remains and is on the point of death. . . ."

Could God be telling me that my work was here behind the Iron Curtain, where His Church was struggling? Was I to have some part in strengthening this thing that remained?

But what could I, one person, do against a force like the one passing in front of me now?

The Cup of Suffering

Our train pulled into Amsterdam right on schedule. I got off carrying a suitcase that was considerably lighter than it had been going to Warsaw.

I did not go directly to Witte. Instead, I went to see the Whetstras in their new Amsterdam home. I told them about my trip. I told them, too, about the Bible verse that had been given to me.

"How would I go about strengthening anything?" I said. "What kind of strength do I have?"

Mr. Whetstra agreed that one lone Dutchman was no answer to the kind of need I described. But Mrs. Whetstra understood.

"No strength at all!" she answered joyously. "Don't you know that it is when we are weakest that God can use us most? Suppose the Holy Spirit has plans behind the Iron Curtain? Talk about strength. . . ."

My return to Witte was coupled with a pleasant surprise.

"Andy," said Geltje. "We have something to show you!"

I followed her into the room that had once been Mama's and Papa's.

"We've decided you should have this for your headquarters."

I never imagined a room of my own in this small house. I knew the sacrifice it was for Arie and Geltje to make me this gift.

"Until you're married!" Papa boomed from the living room. Papa was making frequent remarks about his 27-year-old bachelor son.

That night after the rest of the family had gone to bed, I closed my own door and went around my room feeling my furniture.

"Thank You for a chair, Lord. Thank You for a bureau. . . ." I would build a desk where I could study, work and plan.

I had not been home a week before invitations began to arrive. Churches, clubs, civic groups, schools—everybody wanted to know about life behind the Iron Curtain.

I accepted them all. I certainly needed the payment they offered, but I had a stronger reason. I felt sure that somehow I was going to be shown what I was to do next. And that is what happened.

A church where I was to speak had advertised that my subject was "How Christians Live behind the Iron Curtain." I would never have presumed to speak on such a topic after a three-week visit to one city. But the hall was jammed. And they drew something else: Communists.

I recognized them—some of them had been on the trip. To my surprise, they were quiet during the speech and the question period that followed. But afterward one woman came up to me. She had been a leader of the Dutch delegation in Warsaw.

"I didn't like your talk," she said.

"I'm sorry. I didn't think you would."

"You told only part of the story," she said. "You haven't seen enough. You need to visit more countries, meet more leaders."

What was she leading up to?

"I am in charge of selecting fifteen people from Holland to take a trip to Czechoslovakia. They'll be gone four weeks. There'll be students and professors and people in communications, and we'd like someone from the churches. Would you come?"

Was this God's hand? Was this the next door opening in His plan for me? I decided to put the question before Him once again in terms of money. I knew I didn't have funds for such a trip. "If You want me to go, Lord," I prayed silently, "You'll have to supply the means."

I could feel the lady staring at me.

"For you," she said, "there will be no charge."

So began my second trip behind the Iron Curtain. This group was smaller, and I had trouble getting off by myself. I wondered what God wanted me to learn in Czechoslovakia.

Toward the end of the four weeks I found the answer. Everywhere, we were told about the religious freedom people enjoyed under Communism. Here in Czechoslovakia, our guide said, a group of scholars, paid by the State, had finished a new translation of the Bible. They now were working on a Bible dictionary.

"I would like to visit these men," I said.

I was taken to a large office building in Prague—the Interchurch Center, headquarters for all Protestant churches in Czechoslovakia. I was astonished at the size of the facilities. I was led into a suite of offices where scholarly-looking gentlemen in black coats sat behind heavy tomes and piles of paper. These were the men, I was told, who worked on the new translation. I asked if I might see a copy of the new translation and was shown a bulky, much-fingered manuscript.

"The translation has not been published yet?" I asked.

"No," said one of the scholars. His face seemed sad. "We've had it ready since the war, but . . ." He glanced at the tour director and let his sentence drift off.

"And the Bible dictionary? Is that ready yet?"

"Almost," the scholar blurted out. "It's difficult to find Bibles here nowadays."

I was shepherded out with no chance to ask more questions. But I could see that rather than make an attack on religion, the new regime played the game of frustration. It sponsored a new translation of the Bible—one that never got published. It sponsored a new dictionary of the Bible—but had no Bibles to go with the dictionary.

The next day I asked our guide to take me to the Interdenominational Book Store. I wanted to see how difficult it was to buy a Bible. The shop was well stocked with music, stationery, pictures, statues, crosses and books that were more or less related to religion.

"May I see a red-letter Bible, please?" I asked the saleswoman.

She shook her head. "I'm sorry, sir. Those are out of stock right now."

"How about a black-and-white edition?"

These, too, were temporarily unavailable.

"Ma'am," I said, "I have come all the way from Holland to see how the Church is faring in Czechoslovakia. Are you telling me that in the largest religious bookstore in the country, I cannot buy a Bible?"

The saleswoman disappeared into the back of the store. There was a discussion behind the curtain, followed by the sound of paper rattling. Then the manager himself appeared, carrying a parcel wrapped in brown paper.

"Here you are, sir," the manager said. "That new translation makes Bibles scarce. Until it comes out, new Bibles aren't being printed."

On our last day, we were to go on a tour of model communities. Then we were to come back for dinner, a press conference and final good-byes.

But it was Sunday and my last chance to worship with Czech believers without having a "guide" hovering nearby.

I had been planning my escape for days. I had noticed that the rear door of our tour bus had a faulty spring. Even in "closed" position there was a gap a foot wide between it and the doorjamb.

As the bus pulled away from the hotel that last day, I was in the last seat. At last came a chance when every neck was craned forward, staring at a bronze statue. I squeezed through the opening and stepped down into the street. The bus moved on. I was alone in Prague.

Soon I stood in a church I had spotted on a previous tour of the city. I wondered how a church functioned without Bibles. Occasionally someone carried a hymnal, more rarely a Bible. Many people brought loose-leaf notebooks.

The service began. I took a seat in the back and immediately was surprised. The owners of the hymnbooks held them out at arm's length, high in the air. Those with loose-leaf notebooks did the same. Then I realized the people with books were sharing them with those who had none. In the notebooks were copied, note by note and word by word, the hymns of the congregation.

When the preacher announced a Scripture text, every Bible owner found the reference and held his book high so that friends nearby could follow. I watched them struggling to get close, literally, to the Word. My hand closed over the Dutch Bible in my jacket. I had always taken for granted my right to have this Book. I would never do that again.

After the service I introduced myself to the preacher. When I said I came from Holland chiefly to meet with Christians in his country, he seemed overwhelmed.

"I had heard," he said, "that Czechoslovakia was beginning to open its borders. I didn't believe it. We've been"—he looked around—"almost imprisoned since the war. Please come and talk with me."

Together we went to his apartment. It was only later that I learned how dangerous for him this was in the Czechoslovakia of 1955. He told me the government was trying to get a total grip on the Church. The government selected theological students, choosing only candidates who favored the regime. In addition, every two months a minister had to renew his license. A friend had recently had his renewal application denied—no explanation. Each sermon had to be written out ahead of time and approved by the authorities. Each church had to list its leaders with the State.

It was time for the second service at the church.

"Would you come and speak to us?" he asked.

"Is that possible? Can I preach here?"

"I did not say 'preach.' You can't preach, but you can bring us 'greetings' from Holland. And"—my friend smiled—"if you wish, you could bring us 'greetings' from the Lord."

My interpreter was named Antonin. For a few minutes, I brought greetings from Holland. Then for half an hour I brought greetings to the congregation "from Jesus Christ." Antonin suggested we try it again in another church. That day I visited five churches. Each was memorable in its own way, but the last one most of all.

It was seven p.m., already dark. I knew the tour group would be anxious about me. I needed to find them.

But Antonin asked me if I would visit one more church, "where I think they especially need to meet someone from 'outside.'"

We traveled across Prague to a small Moravian church. There were many people there, around forty of them between the ages of 18 and 25. I spoke my greetings and then answered questions. Could Christians in the Netherlands get jobs? Did anyone report you to the government when you went to church? Could you attend church and still get into a good university?

"You see," Antonin told me, "it's unpatriotic to be a Christian in Czechoslovakia now. Some of these people have been blackballed at work. Many have missed out on education. That"—he held out a small box from a young man who stood beside him—"is why they want you to have this." He went on. "When people in Holland ask you about it, tell them about us and remind them that we are part of the Body, too, and that we are in pain."

I opened the box. Inside was a silver lapel ornament in the shape of a cup. I had seen several wearing this.

Antonin pinned it to my jacket. "This is the symbol of the Church in Czechoslovakia. We call it the Cup of Suffering."

When Antonin left me at the hotel, I found my group was not there—and I didn't know where the farewell dinner was to be held. I went to a restaurant where we had eaten several times. "No, monsieur, the group did not eat here tonight."

The door of the restaurant flew open and the tour director walked in. When she saw me, her shoulders collapsed in relief. Then her face flushed with anger. She indicated the door with a jerk of her head.

Outside at the curb was a government car—a long black limousine with its engine running. The driver got out, opened the door for us and then locked it behind us. We were going to the hotel.

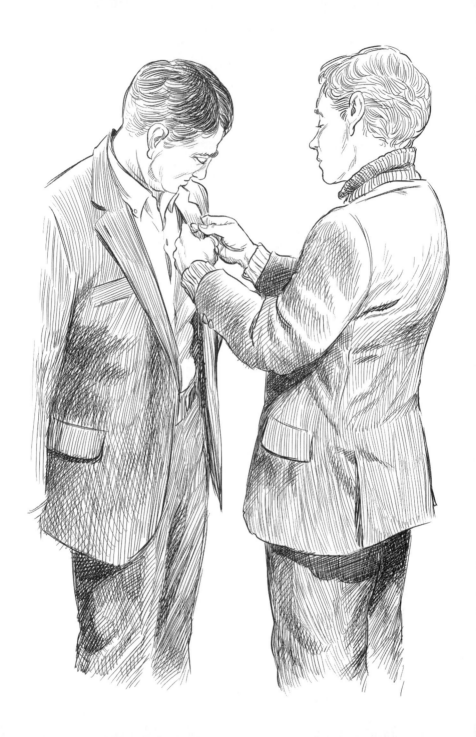

In the car, the tour director spoke. "We have called every hospital, every police station. We finally called the morgue. Where have you been?"

"I got separated," I said, "so I walked around. I'm sorry for the trouble."

"I tell you officially, sir, you are no longer welcome here. You will discover that if you attempt to enter this country again."

Indeed, a year later I applied for a visa to Czechoslovakia and was turned down. It would be five years before I was allowed back inside that beautiful land.

9

Foundations Are Laid

ack home in Witte I made inquiries about return visits and trips to other Iron Curtain countries. I encountered months of questionnaires, delays, forms—but never a visa.

After I returned from Poland, the Dutch magazine *Kracht van Omhoog* asked me to write some articles about my experiences behind the Iron Curtain. As I sat in my room with my empty wallet, I seemed to hear God say, *Write those articles for* Kracht van Omhoog.

I needed money to help with the household. But the magazine offered no payment.

Yet that sense of insistence was there. So I wrote about what I had observed in Poland and in Czechoslovakia. I mailed the articles the next day, and they were published.

Another letter arrived from *Kracht van Omhoog*. Although nowhere in the article had I mentioned money or indicated that I was considering another trip, readers were sending money. The editor wondered where to send it.

So began the amazing story of supply. The first gifts from my unknown friends were small because my needs were small. As my work expanded, contributions from readers increased. Only when there was need for large sums, years later, did God turn elsewhere for our funds.

Then came a letter from a prayer group in Amersfoort. The Holy Spirit, they said, instructed them to get in touch with me; they didn't know why—but could I pay a visit to Amersfoort?

I went to Amersfoort, where a dozen men and women met in the home of a man named Karl de Graaf, a builder of dikes.

I had never met a group like this. These people spent much of their time listening. There was an occasional prayer said aloud around the room, but these prayers were more like outbursts of love and praise for God. Everyone in that room seemed to sense God as very close.

Occasionally, someone apparently heard instruction or information coming from outside his own knowledge. This would be spoken aloud. "Joost's mother, in America, needs our prayers tonight." "We thank You, Lord, that our prayer for Stephje has just now been answered." I was so caught up in this new kind of prayer experience that when it was over, I could scarcely believe it was four-thirty in the morning.

Several days later, I found Karl de Graaf on our front stoop.

"Hello, Andy. Do you know how to drive an automobile?"

"No," I said, bewildered.

"Last night in our prayers we had a word from the Lord about you. It's important you learn to drive."

"Why?" I said.

"Andrew," Mr. de Graaf spoke patiently, "I'm not arguing the logic of this. I'm just delivering the message." With that, he walked back to his waiting car.

A week later Mr. de Graaf was back.

"Have you been taking driving lessons?"

"Well . . . no. . . ."

"Haven't you learned how important obedience is? I suppose I'm going to have to teach you myself. Hop in."

That afternoon I sat behind the wheel of a car for the first time. When I took my driving test a few weeks later, I passed it. I still could see no reason why I should be carrying a driver's license.

"That's the excitement in obedience," Mr. de Graaf said. "Finding out later what God had in mind."

In 1956 came the Hungarian Revolt. Hundreds of thousands of terrified and disillusioned people from Hungary, Yugoslavia, East Germany and other Communist countries fled to the West. These refugees were herded into camps near borders where conditions were unthinkable. In Witte there was a call for volunteers to help in the camps. I was on the first bus.

Volunteers occupied the front of the bus; the back was filled with food, clothing and medicine for the largest refugee camps in West Germany and Austria.

We plunged into a sea of need, passing out clothing and medicine, writing letters, trying to locate separated families, making visa applications. Whenever I could, I held prayer services. And I made an astonishing discovery. Most of the refugees knew literally nothing about the Bible. Older refugees could not read; younger ones raised under Communism were educated but not in the Bible.

Working through interpreters, I held small classes in basic Bible education. I saw people who had been sunk in despair become pillars of strength. I saw bitterness change to hope, shame to pride.

The supplies we brought ran out, and we returned to Holland to collect more. While home, I went to the Yugoslavian consulate to apply again for a visa. This time filling out the paper work, I hesitated on the space for occupation.

What had we learned in Glasgow? Walk in the Light, nothing hidden, everything open and transparent for all to see. So as before, I wrote MISSIONARY.

Our bus was filled again with blankets and clothing, powdered milk, coffee and chocolate for the refugee camps. I was in West Berlin when the telegram came. Papa had died in his garden.

I caught the next train home. I missed the booming voice that had filled the house from floor to rafters. I missed the round-shouldered form bent patiently over rows of cabbages.

I went back to Germany and threw myself harder than ever into the work with the refugees. The West Berlin camps were the saddest, especially its children. I met twelve-year-olds who had never seen the inside of a house. The sick made up 90 percent of every camp.

One day I had the most remarkable impression—as though a voice said, "Today you are going to get the visa for Yugoslavia."

A letter arrived from the Netherlands. In the corner of the envelope was the seal of the Yugoslavian embassy at The Hague.

I ripped the letter open. The Yugoslav government regretted to inform me that my application for a visa had been denied. No explanation.

I had received some kind of message about this letter. But my message had been the visa was granted. Should I go to the Yugoslavian consulate in Berlin and apply?

That is what I did, and once more I came to the line for occupation. This, I suspected, was causing the trouble.

"Lord," I prayed, "what shall I put here?"

I recalled the words of the Great Commission: "Go ye, and teach all nations. . . ."

I wrote TEACHER on the line, handed in the forms and waited.

Twenty minutes later, the clerk came back to wish me a happy journey into his country.

I had to tell someone the news. I got Mr. Whetstra on the telephone.

"Mr. Whetstra. I have in my hand two pieces of paper. One is a letter from the Yugoslavian consulate in The Hague turning down my request for a visa, and the other is my passport, stamped with a visa by the Yugoslav people here.

I've got it, Mr. Whetstra! I'm going behind the Curtain as a missionary!"

"Andrew, you'd better come home for your keys."

"I'm sorry . . . ?"

"To your Volkswagen. Mrs. Whetstra and I decided that if you got the visa, you got our automobile. Come and pick up the keys."

I became the still-unbelieving owner of a blue almost-new Volkswagen.

I spent several days scouring Amsterdam for any kind of Christian printed matter in Yugoslav languages, and going over the car for places to conceal what I found.

I drove to see Karl de Graaf. I could not wait to see his face when he saw the car—visible proof of what he had known by faith.

Mr. de Graaf showed no surprise whatsoever. "Yes," he said, "I thought you'd have it by now." He drew an envelope from his pocket. "God told us you will need an additional sum of money these next two months."

He placed the envelope in my hand. I didn't even open it. By now I knew enough of this remarkable group to know the envelope contained precisely the amount I would need for the trip.

With a heart full of thanks I left Holland for Yugoslavia, behind the Iron Curtain.

Lanterns in the Dark

head was the Yugoslav border. For the first time I was about to enter a Communist country on my own rather than in a group invited by the government.

The Yugoslav government in 1957 permitted visitors to bring in only items for personal use. Anything in quantity was suspect because of the thriving black market. Printed material was confiscated at the border, no matter what quantity, because it was considered foreign propaganda. Here I was with a car and luggage bulging with tracts, Bibles and portions of Bibles. How would I get them past the border guard?

For the very first time, I said the Prayer of God's Smuggler: "Lord, I have Scripture to take to Your children. When You were on earth, You made blind eyes see. Now, I pray,

make seeing eyes blind. Do not let the guards see what You do not want them to see."

I approached the border barrier. Two guards appeared, and one began poking around in my camping gear. In the folds of my sleeping bag and tent were boxes of tracts. "Lord, make seeing eyes blind."

"Do you have anything to declare?"

"I have my money and a wristwatch and a camera. . . ."

The other guard looked inside the VW. He asked me to take out a suitcase in which I had scattered tracts through my clothing. I dragged the suitcase out and opened it. The guard lifted the shirts on top. Beneath them in plain sight was a pile of tracts in two Yugoslavian languages, Croatian and Slovene.

"It seems dry for this time of year," I said to the other guard. Without watching the fellow inspecting the suitcase, I talked about the weather. I talked about my country and how it was always wet on the polders. I could stand the suspense no longer and looked behind me. The guard was not searching my things; he was listening to our conversation.

"Do you have anything else to declare?"

"Only 'small' things," I said. The tracts were small.

The guard nodded to me to close the suitcase and handed back my passport.

My first stop was Zagreb to find a Christian leader there, whom I shall call Jamil. The Dutch Bible Society listed him as a man who ordered Bibles in quantity, but they had not heard from him for many years. I had written a carefully worded letter stating that toward the end of March a Dutchman might visit his country. I drove into Zagreb looking for him.

Later I would learn that my letter was delivered to the address, but Jamil had moved. The new tenant returned the letter to the post office. A lengthy search was made for Jamil's new address. On the very day I entered Yugoslavia, the letter was finally delivered.

Jamil read it, puzzled. Who was this mysterious Dutchman? With a vague feeling nudging him, Jamil went to his old apartment house. He stood on the sidewalk wondering how to proceed.

Soon I pulled up to the curb and stopped my car. Jamil recognized me from my license plates. He seized my hands, overjoyed at having a foreign Christian in his country.

Jamil repeated what I had heard in Poland, that my being there meant everything. Believers felt alone. He would help me contact them in his country. A few days later, with a student named Nikola as my guide and interpreter, I set off in my Volkswagen to bring "greetings" to the Yugoslavian Christians.

My visa was good for fifty days, and for the entire time I preached, taught, encouraged and distributed Scripture. I held more than eighty meetings during those fifty days—speaking sometimes six times on a Sunday.

At first I could not see that the Church in Yugoslavia was under persecution. I had to register with the police when I moved around, but I was free to visit believers. Churches operated openly. Except for certain restricted areas along the borders, I was free to travel within the country, with no government guides checking on me.

This was more freedom than I had expected. But as I got to know Yugoslavia better, I saw the wearing-down process the government exerted on Christians. It centered on the children. Leave old folks alone, but wean young people away from the Church.

Nikola and I visited one church in a village not far from Zagreb. The congregation had not one person under twenty, but Nikola introduced me to a woman who had a ten-year-old son.

"Tell Brother Andrew why Josif is not here," said Nikola.

Her voice was bitter. "The teacher tells my son there is no God. The government tells my son there is no God. They say to Josif, 'Your mama tells you differently, but we know better, don't we? Remember, Mama has no education.' So Josif is not with me."

In Macedonia we encountered signs of fear from its churchgoers. Our first speaking date was scheduled for ten a.m. When we reached the church, not a soul was there.

"I don't understand," Nikola said. "This is the right place."

At eleven we decided to leave. At the car, a villager approached, paused to shake my hand, wished me Godspeed and wandered on. Then another villager approached, and the scene was repeated. For 45 minutes that morning the entire village was out for a stroll, and they all passed the visiting preacher's automobile so they could meet him and shake his hand.

A few days later we had a meeting scheduled in another Macedonian town. The pastor invited us to dinner before the service at eight. At five minutes before eight I suggested we start for the church.

"No," he said. "Not yet."

At 8:15 I brought it up again.

He looked outside before he answered, "No, not yet."

At 8:30 the pastor peered out the window again. "Now we can go," he said. "The people won't come to church until dark."

Then I saw it. In the darkened countryside kerosene lamps appeared. The peasants came across the fields, in twos and threes, never more, each carrying a lamp.

Inside the church, I spoke on Nicodemus. He, too, I said, sought the Lord under cover of darkness. More than two hundred persons came that night to hear the foreigner. Eighty-five of them committed their lives to the Christian way.

In another village in Macedonia we had an encounter with the police.

Nosaki was a small, remote town, and getting there required traveling down muddy tracks with deep ruts, then driving across a plowed field.

The village itself was a collection of mud huts, and we saw no trace of a church. Then Nikola learned that there was in fact a church, but it had only one member. She was the widow Anna, who had converted her home into a church—to which no one came.

We visited Anna. She was amazed to see us.

"But I should not be surprised," she said. "Have I not been praying for help?"

It was forbidden to hold religious services in a private home, so Anna had closed off one room and put a sign on it reading *Molitven Dom* ("Prayer House"). The village's few Party members didn't really object. After all, Anna was alone in her silly superstition.

But now a preacher was here. Word flew from cottage to cottage, and after dark, it looked like the fields were alive with glowworms as peasants with lanterns wove their way to Anna's house. We told them the gospel story; the younger generation had never heard it. We were singing when suddenly there was a loud pounding on the door.

Everyone stopped singing.

Anna opened the door, and there stood two uniformed police. They walked to the front of the room. For a long time they stood there, running their eyes over the congregation. They took out notebooks and wrote down names. They asked questions about Nikola and me. Then they left.

Several villagers went home at once. When the time came for an altar call, I was surprised anyone raised a hand, yet several did.

"You have seen tonight what following Christ might mean," I said. "Are you sure you want to become His people?"

A few insisted. A small church was born that evening, but it never had a chance to grow. Nikola wrote me a year later that it was stamped out by the government. Anna's Molitven Dom was closed.

Roads in Yugoslavia were hard on cars. When we weren't climbing fierce mountain trails, we were fording streams in valleys. Dust from unpaved roads sifted through our closed windows. I hated to think what it was doing to the

engine. Daily, Nikola and I prayed: "Lord, will You please keep the car running?"

In Yugoslavia in 1957, cars were a rarity. When two drivers came upon each other, they stopped to chat about road conditions, weather, gasoline, bridges. One day on a mountain road we spotted a truck approaching up ahead. As it pulled alongside, we stopped.

"Hello," said the driver. "I know who you are. You're the Dutch missionary who is preaching in Terna tonight."

"Yes."

"And this is the Miracle Car?"

"The Miracle Car?"

"The car that you pray for each morning."

I had mentioned the prayer in a meeting; the word had obviously gone on ahead. "Yes." I laughed. "This is the car."

"Mind if I take a look? I'm a mechanic."

"I'd appreciate it." The mechanic lifted the hood. For a long time he stood there, staring.

"Brother Andrew," he said at last, "I have just become a believer. It is mechanically impossible for this engine to run. Look. The air filter. The carburetor. The sparks. This car cannot run."

"And yet it does."

The mechanic shook his head. "Would you permit me to clean your engine and give you an oil change? It hurts to see you abuse a miracle."

That night he took the engine apart, cleaned it, changed the oil and, by the time we were ready to leave the next morning, presented us with an almost new automobile. God answered our prayer.

We drove into Belgrade on May 1, 1957. Nikola and I stood on a church platform, speaking to a crowded room. During the service someone started hammering. The next thing we knew, they had taken a door right off its hinges so an overflow crowd could hear. These were not country people but a sophisticated city congregation.

Nikola and I gave an altar call, asking everyone who wanted to commit their life to Christ, or who wanted to reaffirm a previous commitment, to raise their hand.

Every hand in the room went up.

I explained again how serious a step this was, especially under a hostile government. I made a second appeal, this time asking people to stand.

The entire congregation stood.

Inspired, I launched into an enthusiastic description of daily prayer and Bible reading. A change came over the room. People would not meet my eye.

Puzzled, I turned to the pastor.

"Prayer we can do, yes," he said. "But, Brother Andrew, most people do not have Bibles."

I stared at him in disbelief. In cosmopolitan Belgrade?

I turned to the congregation. "How many of you own Bibles?"

In the entire room seven hands, including the pastor's, went up. I was stunned. I had long ago passed out the ones I had brought with me.

So we worked out a system of Bible-sharing. But that night I promised God that as often as I could lay my hands on a Bible, I would bring it to these children of His behind the wall men had built. How I would buy the Bibles, how I would get them in, I didn't know. I only knew that I would take them to Yugoslavia, to Czechoslovakia and to every other country where God opened the door for me to slip through.

The Prayer

On the way back to Holland, I had time to think and plan. At a rest stop in Germany I got out my Bible. I opened it to the back cover, where I had recorded a prayer that I had made. I remembered the night I had prayed it: "Lord, in a year I'll be thirty. You made a helpmeet for man, but I have not found mine. Lord, I ask You for a wife." I had noted the prayer request in my Bible: *April 12, 1957. Prayed for a wife.*

After Papa's death, I had moved out of the house and into his little room above the toolshed. It had seemed like such a practical idea—the room had a separate entrance, and I could come and go without disturbing the household. But the effect of the move had been to emphasize how very much alone I was.

Back in Witte in July, I prayed again for a wife. "Lord," I said, "I've got to pray again about this bachelor life. A home is where there's a wife and children. Some people are built for the lonely walk. But please, not me."

On a September morning in the middle of my prayer time, a face floated in front of me. Long blond hair. Sunny smile. Eyes never the same shade.

Corry van Dam.

The thought of her came so unexpectedly. Was God showing me the answer to my prayers? It was four years since I left the factory for England and she for nursing school.

Within the hour, I drove to the factory and talked to Mr. Ringers. He said Corry had taken her training at Saint Elizabeth's Hospital in Haarlem and might still be there. If she was married, he had not heard about it. His eyes twinkled.

I telephoned Saint Elizabeth's and held my breath until the receptionist said, "Yes, she's a final-year student. Miss van Dam is living in a private home this year."

I drove to the address and rang the doorbell. A white-haired lady appeared and informed me that Corry's father was seriously ill, and Corry had gone to take care of him. She gave me the address.

A few nights later I stood outside the Van Dam home in Alkmaar, knocking on the door.

Corry opened it. The light behind her turned her hair to gold.

"I've come to ask about your father," I said faintly.

She led me gravely back to her father's room. Mr. van Dam was very ill, but he seemed delighted to have a visitor.

I sat beside his bed and told him about my trips behind the Iron Curtain and my hopes for the future. Corry came and went with bottles and trays, and I tried to keep my eyes from following her. She seemed more heavenly and unattainable than she had been in my dreams.

Twice a week I called on Mr. van Dam. Corry and I held hushed conversations at the front door.

I tried to imagine proposing to Corry. *Please marry me. I'll be gone a lot and you won't know where, and weeks will go by when you won't hear from me. And though we'll be in missionary work, you won't be able to talk about it, and if one time I don't come back, you'll probably never know what happened. No foreseeable income, a single room for a home.*

Who would settle for such a life?

It was during the time I was making these visits that the letter came from the Hungarian consulate. My visa request was approved.

I decided to ask Corry to marry me that very day, but I would not let her answer until I got back from Hungary. This way she would have a taste of the separation, the secrecy, the uncertainty.

I drove to Alkmaar. I pounded on the door, forgetting for a moment the sick man inside. The door opened. One look at Corry's face and I knew.

"Your father—?"

She nodded. "Half an hour ago."

I drove back to Witte with my proposal still burning inside me. After the funeral, I didn't see Corry for three weeks. I spent the time finding every Hungarian-language

Bible I could find and stowing them and a supply of Hungarian tracts in the car.

Finally one moonlit night, I asked Corry to go for a ride. I said everything wrong: "Corry, I want you to marry me, but don't say no until I tell you how hard it will be." I outlined the work I believed God had given me. I told her the next month would be a sample of life for us if she chose to marry me. "You'd be crazy to, Corry," I finished miserably. "But I do so want you to!"

Corry's enormous eyes were bigger still when I finished. She promised she would give me my answer when I returned from Hungary.

At the border crossing in Hungary, once again God made "seeing eyes blind." Soon I was rolling through the countryside, following the beautiful Danube.

I pulled off the road for lunch, drove down a lane and stopped at the water's edge. To get the camp stove out for cooking my lunch, I moved several boxes of tracts the border guards had overlooked.

No sooner had I opened a can of peas and carrots than I heard a roar. A speedboat cut through the water toward me at full throttle. In the bow stood a soldier with a drawn machine gun. The boat swerved and coasted to a landing at the river's edge, and I saw two other soldiers in the boat. Two of them leaped ashore.

"Lord," I prayed, "help me refuse to yield to fear."

The first soldier kept the machine gun on me while the other ran to my car. I stirred peas and carrots as I watched him open the door.

I began speaking Dutch, which I felt sure these men would not understand.

"It's nice to have you drop in."

The soldier stared stonily.

"As you can see, I'm preparing to eat."

Behind me I heard the other car door open. "Would you care to join me?" I raised my eyebrows and waved my hand in a gesture of invitation. The soldier shook his head brusquely. The other soldier poked around the car.

"Well, I'm going to eat while the food is hot." I spooned the vegetables onto my plate. In a gesture far more deliberate than normal, I bowed my head, folded my hands and prayed aloud a long thanksgiving for the food I was about to eat.

There was no sound from the soldiers. As I finished praying, the door slammed and I heard boots come rapidly toward me. I picked up my fork and took a bite. For a moment both soldiers stood there. Then abruptly they whirled. Without looking back, they ran to their boat, jumped in and roared off.

Budapest was a lovely city, but the signs of revolt were everywhere—buildings pockmarked with bullet holes, trees ripped up, tram rails twisted.

I had the address of Professor B, a man who held an excellent position in a famous school in Budapest. When I asked him to be my interpreter, he said, "Of course, Brother. We are in this together." That decision would cost my friend his livelihood.

Professor B was overjoyed with the Bibles. He said they were almost unattainable. He told me that there were many churches open and functioning as best they could. I could be as busy as I chose, speaking and distributing Bibles, provided I didn't mind taking a few risks.

"A few risks?" I said.

"The authorities think every church supper is hatching a plot." Those who suffered most, he said, were the pastors. Most of those in Budapest had been in serious trouble with the regime: About a third had spent time in prison, some for as long as six years. Each preacher had to have his permit renewed every two months. This regulation kept them in constant tension.

Professor B took me to visit a pastor friend of his. The man opened the door cautiously and looked up and down the hall before letting us in. His apartment was filled with lampshades. I learned he had been dismissed from his pulpit—no reason given. In order to keep his family from starving, he painted lampshades from early morning until late at night.

I asked Professor B how typical this pastor's plight was.

"Fairly typical among the churches that do not compromise," he said. But some churches in Hungary found ways around their restrictions. He asked me one morning to take part in a Hungarian wedding.

"This will be like no wedding you've attended," he promised. "You will be asked to speak. Say a quick word of congratulation to the bride and groom. Then preach the hardest-hitting sermon we can pray for."

I had to smile.

"Don't laugh," said Professor B. "People are afraid to enter a church these days except for funerals and weddings.

So we preach to them then! A government official said to me last week, 'I'll bet every night you pray for your friends to die so you can get your sermon in.'"

So I preached at the wedding. Afterward I told Professor B about bringing "greetings" from Holland. He liked the idea and began making calls. That night we held a revival meeting in one of the largest churches in town.

The next night we held another meeting in a different church. And so on, night after night. We never announced where the next meeting would be. Even so, the word got out; people lined up on the sidewalk to hear the visiting Dutchman talk.

This attracted attention. As we sat on platforms waiting for services to begin, I would see the pastors searching the faces in the congregation.

"They're looking for the secret police," Professor B explained. "We know many of them by sight. After the revolt it has been dangerous to attract large crowds for any reason."

One evening the police came. I knew it from Professor B's face.

"They're here," he whispered. He signaled that I was to follow him back into the vestry. Two plainclothesmen were waiting. They asked me questions, then issued a summons for me to appear the following morning, along with Professor B, at headquarters.

"The last time this happened," Professor B said later, "two men went to prison for a long time."

After the service all the pastors gathered in the vestry. Professor B suggested we go to his home and pray. It was

the first time I had been to his house, and it was luxurious. It showed the prominent position he risked.

Professor B introduced me to his son, Janos. He was a young attorney, and he, too, was willing to place his career on the line by taking part in these frowned-upon meetings. There were seven of us that night, gathered in much the same way Christians had gathered since the Church began—in secret, in trouble—praying together that through the miraculous intervention of God Himself we be spared a confrontation with the authorities.

We all knelt around a low round table in Professor B's living room. For an hour we begged God to help us in our time of need. All at once, the praying stopped. To each of us at the same instant came the inexplicable certainty that our prayer was answered.

We blinked at each other in surprise. I looked at my watch—11:35 p.m. At that precise hour we *knew* that tomorrow everything was going to be all right.

The next morning promptly at nine, Professor B and I were at headquarters. Professor B knew the staff well. The department head was unrelenting in his attacks on the Church; his deputy was more likely to be lenient.

"We are scheduled," Professor B said, "to see the department head. Too bad."

Nine-thirty came, and then ten o'clock. Eleven. Just before noon, a clerk took us down a long corridor. We passed the department head's office and kept going. Professor B glanced at me. At last we stopped, and the clerk explained that the head of the department had fallen ill the night before. The deputy would hear our case.

Twenty minutes later we left the office, free men. I yearned to ask the clerk at what hour the department head had fallen ill. To this day I believe his answer would have been 11:35 p.m.

The encounter with the authorities ended further meetings in Budapest for the time being. Professor B arranged a ten-day speaking tour for me in eastern Hungary and found an interpreter to go with me.

When I returned, I went to see Janos and Professor B. Right away I knew something was wrong. Both were at home in the middle of the day, though neither let on that all was not well. They invited me to have breakfast with them the next morning before I started home.

The next morning I sensed again something was wrong. As we finished breakfast, Janos drew a small package from his pocket. It was only later that the full impact of his words would become clear.

"We have so little way of saying thank-you," said Janos. "You risk much coming to our country. We want you to take this to that girl back in Holland."

I had told them about Corry. Inside the box was an antique gold pin, set with rubies. They laughed at my expression. "We're praying," Janos said, "that the answer's going to be yes."

I was halfway across Austria on my way home, camping in my tent, when I woke up in the middle of the night with a terrifying nightmare. I was being chased by a squadron of police in red scarves who were clapping, clapping, clapping.

Somehow I knew that it had something to do with Professor B; I was sure he was in danger. The next day, I sent him a letter.

In Holland I drove straight to the hospital in Haarlem. I was waiting for Corry when she came out from working the night shift. Under the streetlight her hair was copper instead of gold.

"I'm back, Corry," I said. "And I love you whether the answer is yes or no."

Corry laughed. "Oh, Andy!" she said. "I love you, too! I'm going to worry about you, miss you and pray for you, no matter what. So shouldn't I be a worried wife rather than a cranky friend?"

"Corry," I said, not knowing that I was saying for the first time words that would become a motto for us, "we don't know where the road leads, do we?"

"But, Andy," she said, "let's go there together."

Back at Witte, there was a letter from Professor B. He thanked me once again for coming to Hungary, and he hoped I would come again. He wrote:

I believe I should share with you something that has happened. Do not think it is the result of your visit—it was coming anyhow. I have been forced to resign from the university. Do not feel sad. Many have given up far more for their Savior.

Do not be sidetracked from this important work of encouragement. That is your task, as we have ours. We pray daily for you, although you will not hear from us anymore. This is being carried from the country by a friend. Our mail is censored. We pray that your ministry continue strong.

Once again, you must not be downcast. We praise the Lord.

12

Counterfeit Church

Corry and I were married in Alkmaar on June 27, 1958, with family and friends there to celebrate with us. It was dark before we could tear ourselves away.

For the honeymoon we borrowed Karl de Graaf's house trailer. We talked about driving to France. But setting out, we realized how tired we were, Corry from her final examinations, I from the work in the refugee camps where I spent most of my time during our engagement. A few miles from Alkmaar we came to a restaurant in a grove of trees and went in for coffee. So cordial were the owner and his wife, so insistent that the trailer was no trouble, that that was as far as we got. We pulled the trailer deep under the trees and spent our honeymoon right there.

My single room above the toolshed was now filled with sunshine and warmth. Corry made it home.

We didn't have a kitchen. There was no plumbing in our home. The roof leaked here and there, never two nights in the same place. What did it matter as long as we were together?

The only real problem was the clothing bundles. I had talked in churches all over Holland about the need for clothes in the refugee camps and suggested my address as a place to send them. I never dreamed how much would come! Load after load was deposited in the front yard— eight tons of it that first year. The problem of storage was acute. There was no place for the clothes but our one room. I packed the car as full as I could each time I left for the camps, but the Volkswagen made an unsatisfactory truck.

I was eager for Corry to see the camps for herself, not only so that she would meet the people, but because I knew what a nurse could mean there. That fall we piled the backseat with sweaters and coats and shoes and set out together for the camps in West Berlin.

We delivered the first load to an old military barracks used by the Nazis during the war and now converted into "homes" for refugees. It was Corry's first glimpse of the squalor of the camps. That night she could not eat. But the next day, she started helping.

During this trip I knew I needed to visit East Germany. West Berlin was the obvious point of departure. But when I proposed the trip to Corry, she looked at me with stricken eyes.

"Oh, Andy!" she said. "How can I leave? There's so much to do here!"

I looked at her closely: Her cheeks were flushed, her eyes glazed. I wondered if I had been wrong to bring her here. For a nurse—trained to see what should be done but without facilities to do it—it was torture. She moved from camp to camp, setting up tanks for boiled water, and at one place trying to get the dishes of those who had tuberculosis handled separately from the dishes of those who did not. She painted feverish throats with medicine, cleaned sores, washed infected eyes, even on occasion pulled teeth.

For her own sake I wanted to get her away from this environment. But she refused. "You go," she said when the visas for East Germany came through. "I can't preach. I can't speak German. I can't even drive a car. But I can spot a toilet crawling with germs when I see one." She picked up the disinfectant that was never far from her side. "Tell me about it when you get back."

I crossed over from West to East Berlin, and the difference between the two halves of the city was observable even as I drove down the streets. Nobody talked in the streets. There were police everywhere, stopping people at random, searching briefcases, shopping bags, pocketbooks.

The government presence was on the radio, loudspeakers, billboards. There was propaganda everywhere.

East Germany was going through a devastating food shortage.

What did the government do? Signs appeared, along with radio announcements and newspaper advertisements: "Don't let anyone tell you there is a bread shortage. There is plenty of bread. This is another example of the victory of socialism over the forces of nature."

Only there was no bread. I went into grocery stores and found none. Even restaurants didn't have any.

The saddest part was that no one talked about the missing bread. The people were silent.

The part of East Germany I was interested in was southern Saxony. Refugees said the Church was alive there. I was not prepared for *how* alive.

A man whose name I had been given, Wilhelm, was a youth worker for the Lutheran Fellowship. He and his wife, Mar, lived in a hilly, wooded section. A motorbike carried Wilhelm all over East Germany in sun, snow and rain.

Wilhelm met me at the door and invited me in. We sat around their kitchen table drinking coffee while I explained my mission behind the Curtain.

"I'm glad you've come," said Wilhelm. He stopped to cough, a deep dry cough that racked his whole frame. "We need all the encouragement we can find."

"Do you need Bibles?" I asked.

"We have Bibles."

"You said you needed encouragement?"

Then I learned how the Communists had chosen not to persecute the Church but rather to persuade young people away from it with emotional patriotism and celebratory ceremonies, alternatives to baptisms and christenings. In essence, they were offering a counterfeit church.

Wilhelm planned a tour of several churches. I suggested we go in my car, and Mar smiled at me gratefully. "It's that awful motorbike that makes him cough," she said. "Thousands of kilometers in all kinds of weather."

In the car, Wilhelm said, "I am so glad you have come to be with us. You help us remember that the Church is larger than any one political scene. With God on our side, we shall conquer."

For nearly two weeks I traveled with him throughout East Germany, preaching with an amazing freedom to churches that had plenty of Bibles, plenty of literature, wide open meetings—and that were demoralized beyond any churches I had yet met behind the Curtain.

During those twelve days, I preached one sermon over and over. I urged the German Christians to become missionaries.

At the first church the pastor stood up and said, "Brother Andrew, it's easy for you to speak about missionary work, because you can travel anywhere you want. But what about us here in East Germany? We can't even leave the country."

"Wait!" I said. "Think about what you said. I must take a long and costly trip to get to Eastern Europe. But you're already here! How many Russian soldiers are there in your country now? How many unconverted fellow Germans are there? God is bringing the mission field to you!"

I spoke of the time Paul was in prison in Rome chained between two soldiers. "Paul thanked God that he had a captive audience. He began to preach the Gospel. After a while the guard was changed; two more soldiers came in. Paul thanked God for the two new ones and began again. The result was that he made these men Christians right there in Caesar's household.

"This is the mission of Christians behind the Curtain."

The Inner Circle

Back in West Berlin, I found Corry conducting lice inspection on the children. I was appalled at the change in her. She had lost weight, her skin had a yellowish pallor, there were circles under her eyes. I accused myself for having left her alone.

I wanted to try to take Bibles into Yugoslavia from Berlin. I knew from previous experience that their consulate in Berlin was the place to apply for the visa, rather than The Hague.

Now, as I looked at my young wife, I realized that a trip to Yugoslavia would serve a double purpose. What better place to forget the camps than that beautiful land? I took both our passports to the Yugoslav consulate and spent the rest of the day buying Bibles. Soon Corry and I set out together for the Iron Curtain.

If it had not been for Corry's illness, that first week of the trip would have been perfect. The border guards spotted us for newlyweds. I filed away this knowledge: A man and a woman together raised less suspicion than a man traveling alone.

Jamil and Nikola greeted us joyfully. When we brought the new Bibles out in church after church, the congregations could scarcely believe their eyes. The women kissed Corry, the men thumped me on the back.

For six days, with Nikola interpreting, I shared with Yugoslavian churches the vision I had in East Germany—of Iron Curtain churches not in retreat but on the advance.

On the evening of the seventh day, while we were eating dinner in the house of friends, the police came. Corry didn't feel well and had gone to lie down. There was a knock on the door, and in walked two gray-uniformed police.

"Come with us," they said to me.

I looked at my friends, who sat, forks raised, mouths open in fear. Corry appeared in the doorway.

"She is with you?"

"Yes."

"Her too."

The police knew all about my former trip to Yugoslavia. They informed us that we would have to leave the country immediately. My visa had been canceled. Would I please hand over my passport.

I turned over my papers. The officers took out an enormous red stamp, which they slammed down across my visa. I was *persona non grata* in Yugoslavia.

Corry was shaken. "Andy, I was scared stiff!" she said as we drove across Austria toward Germany.

We intended to stop in Berlin briefly. I wanted to get Corry home and to a doctor. Something was wrong. Frequently I had to stop the car and let her stretch full length on the grass until the retching sickness passed.

In Berlin was a surprise. Since the Yugoslav consulate there was more lenient than the one in The Hague, I had made the rounds of the Berlin offices of every country I wanted to visit. Now two letters waited for me at the hostel. Both Bulgaria and Romania were pleased to tell me to appear at their Berlin headquarters to have my travel documents validated.

Bulgaria and Romania! Two of the countries where persecution of the Church was most intense—what I called the Inner Circle!

But Corry needed her own bed. And there was that stamp in my passport. The other governments would want to know why I had been expelled from Yugoslavia.

So we went directly home to Witte. Corry went to bed, and I called the doctor.

"Your wife is fine," he said after examining her. "I've given her pills for the nausea, and she should see me next month."

"But what's the matter with her?"

The doctor held out his hand. "Congratulations. You're going to be a father."

We had returned from the trip in November. The baby was due in June. By January, Corry was feeling so well that I began to think again about that trip into the Inner Circle—by myself. I would be back in plenty of time for the baby's birth.

But the passport. What could I do about the bad page?

I went to The Hague's office of passport control and showed the reviewing officer my problem. "I sympathize with you," he said, "but there's nothing we can do."

"I'm a missionary," I said. "I want to go to these countries to contact the Christians there."

He considered this. He shook his head. "We can't even give you hints about how to get a new passport quickly. Such as, for instance, doing a lot of travel to nearby countries and always insisting that they stamp your papers, so that your passport will fill up sooner. We couldn't even give you hints like that. I'm very sorry."

Within a few weeks I had a new passport.

Corry helped me stow Bibles in the car. "Bulgaria and Romania," she said softly. "We want you back, Andrew, your baby and I."

I tried to reassure her as I climbed into the loaded car.

"You've got your money?" Corry asked.

I felt my wallet. For once I was going with more than enough. I could not understand why so many gifts had come from readers of *Kracht van Omhoog* lately. It cost me very little to travel, sleeping in the tent, fixing my own meals. I had tried to leave the extra amount with Corry, but she had insisted that I take it with me.

With a last kiss I was off.

I headed from the Austrian camp toward Yugoslavia, the country from which I had recently been expelled. But there was no other practical route into Bulgaria. The only other way to go would be a long trip the length of Italy, by boat to Greece and then a long drive up through Greek Macedonia.

There had been no trouble getting a new visa. Yugoslavian paper work was notoriously inefficient, and the Western consulates had not learned about my problem. The only place there might be trouble, I thought, was at the border itself.

Once there, however, the guard only glanced at my passport, and within twenty minutes I was across.

I had now four days of grace in Yugoslavia before the information about my arrival at the border was checked against the unwanted persons file in Belgrade. I stopped for a brief visit with Jamil and then pressed on, intending to cross the border into Bulgaria on the morning of the fifth day. Jamil supplied me with enough names and churches along my route to have kept me busy for a month. There had not been any trouble from the authorities. I decided to stay another 24 hours.

On the fifth evening I checked into a hotel after midnight and turned in my passport at the desk. I had slept for perhaps five hours when there was an abrupt rap on the door. I found two men in suits standing in the hall.

"Dress and follow us," they said.

I struggled into pants and a shirt. We walked through the lobby. Outside, we walked a few hundred yards to a large stone building. I was shepherded into an office.

The man behind the desk had my passport in his hand.

"Why are you back in Yugoslavia?" he demanded. "How did you get this passport changed? Is this what your country does, make it easy for lawbreakers?"

He took out the enormous stamp with the red ink. He slammed it down on the Yugoslav visa three times.

"You will leave the country within twenty-four hours," he said. "We will telephone the border guard in Trieste when to expect you."

Trieste was right back where I had come from, while here we were fifty miles from the Bulgarian border.

"I'm on my way to Bulgaria!" I pleaded. "Couldn't I leave the country that way?"

He was adamant. Trieste, and as quickly as possible.

With a sinking heart, I headed back to Trieste and the long roundabout trip through Italy and Greece—fifteen hundred miles out of my way.

A depression I had never known before settled over me as I inched my way down the boot of Italy. Corry's first birthday since we were married came and went, and I was not even out of Italy. Suppose there was trouble with the police in Bulgaria. Suppose I didn't get back for the birth of the baby. I understood now the reason for the extra money.

To make matters worse, there was that stamp on the Yugoslavia page again.

Then my back began to act up. For three or four years I had had trouble on and off with a slipped disk. It bothered me most when I drove long distances. About halfway through Italy the trouble began again, worse than I had ever known. By the time I reached the boat for Greece, I was literally bent double.

When I took the car off the boat in Greece, I was no better; after a couple of days on Greek roads, I was literally crying with pain. The Greek roads were rocks and chuckholes. I could not read the signs in the Greek alphabet, and often I would make a wrong turn and have to turn back.

Then I learned that the border crossing toward which I had been heading was open to diplomats only. For ordinary travelers there was no entry at all into Bulgaria from Greece. The only way was through Turkey, many miles and many days away.

The morning after this discovery I was bumping along a stony road, when up ahead I saw a blue sign:

FILIPPI

I stopped the car with a jerk. Philippi? From the Bible? The town where Paul and Silas had been in prison—where God sent the earthquake to open the door?

Yes! This was the place! I got out of the car and stared at a field of ruins, old streets, what was left of a temple, a row of houses, only the walls standing now.

Paul had been in prison in this place. Now I was in a prison of pain and discouragement. Paul and Silas had been doing what I was doing, preaching the Gospel where it was not allowed. God performed a miracle to get His men out of prison. In that instant I knew that He was performing another one to get me out of mine.

The bonds of depression that had wrapped themselves around me snapped like the chains on Paul's wrists. The heaviness lifted, and as it did I realized I was standing upright, head high. Joy welled up in me.

I literally ran back to the car. I started the engine and with a roar set off once more for the unknown believers of the Inner Circle.

Abraham the Giant Killer

At the border crossing from Turkey into Bulgaria, the customs inspector did not ask me to open anything. He entered the date and point of entry on my Bulgarian visa but did not turn the other pages in the passport. Then he made a little speech in English welcoming me to the country.

The Bulgarian highway was newly paved. All along it children shouted and ran along the edge of the road. Men and women working in the fields straightened up to smile and wave, a thing I had not seen anywhere else in Europe.

That first evening I turned up a mountainside and found a camping site. In the morning I spent some time repacking Bibles. Then I drove down the mountain, slipping and sliding on a gravel road. I soon found myself on a track in the backyards of a village. The road was getting muddier.

I splashed through a little stream, and a few feet farther on I bogged down altogether.

There I sat. What was I going to do?

I heard loud singing coming from a building on the edge of the village. I got out and slogged through the muck until I reached the building.

It was a pub, and although it was only ten in the morning, the sounds were those of drinking men. I stepped inside. Instantly the singing stopped.

Twenty faces stared at me, a foreigner in their village.

"Does anyone here speak English?" I asked. No one responded. "German?" No. "Dutch?"

"Well, hello anyway," I said, smiling and touching my forehead in salute. While these round, brown-eyed faces stared at me, I went into a pantomime routine. I made a noise that was meant to sound like a car getting stuck in the mud. I held my hands out like a man holding a steering wheel with both hands.

"Ahh!" The man behind the bar nodded knowingly and ran to me with two glasses of beer, shoving one in each outstretched hand.

"No, no," I said, laughing. I put the glasses down and signaled with my arm. "Come!"

Several men rose from their tables, and I felt like the Pied Piper leading the parade to my blue VW in the mud.

"Ahh!" Nodding of heads. Now they understood! In their knee-high boots, they waded into the mud, indicating that I should get behind the wheel. These broad-shouldered men lifted, and within moments we were on the main road in front of the pub.

I got out of the car and thanked them. I took one work-hardened hand after the other, shook it soundly and moved on.

"I thank you," I said. "Holland thanks you. The Lord thanks you. . . ."

One man did not let go of my hand. Instead he pulled me with him into the pub. I knew what was going to happen. They were going to buy me a beer whether I wanted one or not.

I had not had a drink since more than nine years before, when I turned my will over to God. "What should I do now, Lord?" I asked aloud in Dutch. And suddenly I knew that I had to go ahead and drink that beer, that to turn it down would be to turn them down, that their kindness and hospitality ranked higher with God than following a rule.

Twenty minutes later, eyes watering from the homemade brew, I once again shook twenty hands, wished them the speediest of all possible salvations and went on my way.

In Yugoslavia, I had met a man whose closest friend, Petroff, lived in Sofia, Bulgaria. "Will you go to see him?" he asked.

Of course I would.

Sofia was beautiful. Early the next morning I left the hotel and headed for the street where Petroff lived. I found it easily and began looking for the number.

As I walked along the sidewalk, a man came down the street from the opposite direction. We drew abreast just as I came to the number I was looking for. It was an apartment house. I turned up the walkway, and so did the stranger!

I glanced for a second into the face of the man who had arrived at the precise moment I did. I experienced one of the miracles of the Christian life: Our spirits recognized each other.

Without a word we marched side by side up the stairs. The stranger reached his apartment, took out his key and threw open the door. Without invitation I walked into his house. Quickly, he closed the door behind him. We faced each other in the single room that was his home.

"I am Andrew from Holland."

"And I," he said, "am Petroff."

Petroff and his wife lived in this single room. The three of us spent our first few moments together thanking God for having brought us together in this wonderful way.

Then we talked. "I've heard," I said, "that both Bulgaria and Romania are desperately in need of Bibles. Is that so?"

Petroff walked me to his desk. An ancient typewriter with a sheet of paper in it sat next to a Bible, open to Exodus.

"Three weeks ago," said Petroff, "I managed to find this Bible." He showed me a second volume on the dining table. "I got it cheap because the books of Genesis, Exodus and Revelation have been cut out."

"Why?"

"Who knows? Perhaps to sell. Or to make cigarettes with the thin paper. I was lucky enough to have the money to purchase it. When I fill in the missing parts from my own Bible, I will have another complete book! I ought to be finished in four weeks."

"What will you do with the second Bible then?"

"Give it to a church," said his wife, "where there's no Bible."

No Bible in the entire church?

"There are many such churches in this country," said Petroff. "It's the same in Romania and in Russia. Since Communism, it's been impossible to buy them."

I could hardly wait to show Petroff the treasure I had for him in my car.

That night I drove to the apartment, checked the street to make sure it was empty and then took inside a carton of Bibles. Petroff and his wife watched me put the box on their table, their eyes wide in curiosity.

I lifted the top and took out a Bible. I put it in the hands of Petroff and another into the hands of his wife.

"And in the box?" Petroff asked.

"More. And still more outside."

Petroff closed his eyes. Two tears rolled slowly out from between his closed lids and fell on the volume in his hands.

Petroff and I set off immediately on an extended trip through Bulgaria, delivering the Bibles to churches where he knew the need was greatest.

In my first service of worship in Bulgaria, it took twelve people more than an hour to assemble in an apartment, arriving at intervals so that it would not appear that a group was gathering. Blankets had been draped over the window to block out prying eyes. Each new worshiper took a place around the central table, bowed his or her head and prayed silently for the safety of the meeting. At eight o'clock Petroff stood up and spoke in a low voice, translating for me as he went.

"We are blessed tonight to have a brother visit us from Holland," Petroff whispered. "I shall ask him to share with you a message from the Lord."

I spoke for twenty minutes, then nodded to Petroff. With a flourish, he unwrapped a package and held up . . . a Bible!

There were great bear hugs from the men and warm foreheads-on-the-shoulder from the women, before they passed the Book from one hand to another, tenderly opening it and closing it again.

We separated as we had come, in ones and twos, at intervals, for over an hour. The last person to get up from his knees was a grizzly bear of a man with a beard and the kindest blue eyes I had ever seen. This, Petroff told me, was Abraham.

Abraham lived in a tent in the mountains. At one time he had owned land but had lost it because of his "subversive" activities.

"Someday you must visit him in his home," Petroff said. It will show you what a man will sacrifice in the name of his God." Most of the year, he said, Abraham and his wife lived on wild berries and bread.

Petroff called Abraham the Giant Killer, because he was always setting out to find his "Goliath"—some high-ranking Party official or army man to whom he could bring his witness. "Abraham is always seeking a new Goliath," Petroff said. "He finds him, and then there is a fight. Goliath wins, and Abraham ends up in jail. But on many occasions Abraham wins a new soul to Christ."

I went to my car and brought Abraham the Giant Killer the rest of the Bulgarian Bibles. He would know what to do with them.

Abraham held the Bibles as he might hold a baby. His blue eyes burned into mine as Petroff translated for him.

"The front line is long, Brother. Here we must give a little, there we may advance. This day, Andrew from Holland, we have made an advance."

The rest of that first trip to Bulgaria was spent visiting underground churches. "Strengthen the things that remain" became more than ever a command that haunted my sleep. How courageous they were, this remnant of the Church.

I learned another thing. No matter how dead, no matter how subservient a church may appear on the surface, it had God's eye upon it.

Before I left Bulgaria, Petroff and I drove into the mountains to find Abraham. We had no idea how to locate his tent, only the name of the village nearest to it. The road finally vanished altogether. We got out and stood, undecided, beside the town's artesian well. Above us the forest stretched as far as we could see. Where in that wilderness was the man we were looking for?

The people at the well stared at us curiously as they waited to fill their jars. Then the first man in line finished drinking, straightened up and turned around. It was Abraham himself!

His blue eyes blazed like the sky at noonday. Suddenly I was drowning in a mammoth wet embrace, the icy water on his great beard drenching me. Abraham was even more astonished than we at this unplanned meeting; he came to the village only every fourth day, long enough to buy bread. He picked up half a dozen loaves now from the stone wall beside the well and began leading us up the mountainside.

For two hours we climbed. Abraham had just returned the week before from giving away the last of the Bibles, and he described in detail how they were received.

Finally we rounded a rocky ledge, stepped behind some pines and found Abraham's goatskin tent. His wife stepped outside. She was as tiny as her husband was big, with skin like wrinkled parchment. Their eyes were alike, blue, trusting. I looked at this woman who once had a house filled with rugs, linens and even servants, for they had been well-to-do; I thought I had never seen a face more content.

She offered us blackberries and wild honey. We ate little, not knowing how much they had, and we stayed only a short while because we didn't care to go down the mountain after dark. In those moments was forged a friendship that is one of the bulwarks of my life.

The Romanians

It took me four hours to get across the Romanian border. When I pulled up to the checkpoint at the Romanian border, I said to myself, "Only a few cars. This will go swiftly."

But after forty minutes, the first car was still being inspected. When that car finally left and the next inspection took half an hour, I began to worry. Literally everything that family carried was taken out and spread on the ground. The next car went through the same routine. The fourth inspection lasted over an hour. The guards took the driver inside while they removed hubcaps, took his engine apart, removed seats.

"Dear Lord," I said, when there was just one car ahead of me, "no amount of cleverness on my part will get me across

this border. Dare I ask for a miracle? Let me take out some Romanian Bibles and leave them in the open where they will be seen. Then, Lord, I cannot possibly depend upon myself; I depend utterly upon You."

While the last car went through its chilling inspection, I took several Bibles from their hiding places and piled them on the seat beside me.

It was my turn. I inched up to the officer standing at the side of the road, handed him my papers and started to get out. But his knee was against the door, holding it closed. He looked at my passport photograph, scribbled something down, shoved the papers back under my nose and waved me on.

I started the engine. Was I supposed to pull over? I inched forward, my foot poised above the brake. I looked out the rear mirror. The guard waved the next car to a stop, indicating to the driver to get out. I drove a few more yards. The guard had the driver behind me open his hood.

I had made it through that checkpoint in the space of thirty seconds.

In Romania, I sensed a new degree of police control. At nearly every village, there was a police checkpoint, stopping every peasant on his bicycle. Where was he going? What was his business? Even I, a "tourist," had my visa stamped with the cities I would visit and dates on which I must appear at each point along my itinerary. Once, I arrived in a town about fifty miles from Cluj and decided, since it was late, that I would like to spend the night there. The local authorities were surprised.

"Sir," they said, looking at my tourist card, "you are expected for dinner in Cluj. You can make it now by hurrying."

So I sped into Cluj, arriving just as the hotel dining room was closing, to find my table set, hors d'oeuvres out and a little Dutch flag sitting in the center of the table.

Inside the various cities, I was free to come and go as I chose. My first Sunday morning, I woke early, anxious to join my fellow Christians in this lovely land.

The chief weapon against the Church in Romania was something called Consolidation. Wherever there were churches with empty pews, the congregations were merged with others in nearby villages. The leftover facilities were confiscated by the State. That meant many members of shut-down churches simply ceased attending anywhere. Most were peasants, and travel between villages was slow and difficult.

Two church services were allowed each week, one on Saturday, another on Sunday. But Saturday was a workday in Romania, and Saturday night services were poorly attended. So in effect, worship had been consolidated into a single Sunday meeting.

But what a meeting!

I arrived at ten on Sunday morning to a service that had already been underway for an hour. I would not have found a place to sit, except that I was recognized as a foreigner and invited to take a seat on the dais. I spent three hours with these Christians in the heart of Communism's Inner Circle.

When it came time for the collection, I put in the plate approximately the amount in Romanian currency that I would have at home. I was the first person to whom the plate was passed: There lay my bill for all to see.

As the collection continued, I realized with embarrassment that I had put in twenty or thirty times as much as anyone else. I noticed something else. Often someone would put a coin in the basin and hold it while he made change. A bill as large as the one I placed in the plate probably represented a month's income. I felt bad about coming across as a rich foreigner.

To make matters worse, the head usher, instead of taking the plate to the altar, brought it to *me*! I was to take my change. What should I do?

With every eye in the room upon me, I suddenly realized with great joy that this was not my money at all. "That was not from me," I said in German—fortunately a man in the congregation translated. I remembered the generous readers of *Kracht van Omhoog*. "It is a gift from the believers in the Netherlands to the believers in Romania. It is a token of oneness in the Body of Christ."

I watched the faces in the room as the man translated. Again I saw that dawning hope: We are not alone? We have friends we never knew in other places?

After the service broke, I approached the man who had spoken German and said that I would like to talk with him. It turned out that he was secretary for the entire denomination in Romania. But he did not want to talk to me privately at all. When I pushed a bit, he agreed to have me come to the denomination's office the next day. "I will see that the president is there for a brief talk with you," he said.

The next day I walked into the headquarters of this denomination, carrying six Bibles in my briefcase. The secretary from the day before was there, looking uncomfortable. Big drops of perspiration had formed on his forehead. I could not get over the impression that he was in terror of something or someone.

I was ushered into the office of the president. "What can I do for you?" he asked in German.

I shook his hand. I told him I was visiting his country as a Christian and wanted to bring back to my people any word of greeting he might like to extend.

His face relaxed. A word of greeting to the exploited peoples of Holland from the people of the great Republica Populars of Romina! The secretary stopped mopping his forehead.

"Won't you sit down?" he asked. We talked about Romanian tomatoes, the largest I had ever seen, and about watermelon, which I tasted for the first time in this country. We talked about the climate, kept mild by the Black Sea.

Eventually the conversation lagged. I decided the time had come either to be rebuffed or to establish a real contact with these two frightened men.

I opened my briefcase and drew out one of the Bibles. "Will you permit the Dutch people to present the Romanian people with these copies of the Bible?"

Right away the two men stiffened. The secretary began to perspire again. The president took the Bible in his hand, and for the briefest moment I caught the tenderness with which he held it.

But he shoved the Bible back into my hands.

"I do not want this," he said.

I left carrying the six Bibles I had come in with.

For the following week I met Christians living under persecution, but who had kept alive some divine hope. Whenever I met with the leaders of established Protestant denominations in their official headquarters, there were two men present besides myself. Suspicion of one's fellow Christians played a large part in wearing down the Church.

I worried about the president of one denomination—Gheorghe—the moment he stepped into the room. He was so winded from walking that it was several minutes before he could catch his breath.

We discovered a problem. Neither he nor Ion, secretary of the group, spoke a word of my languages, nor I of theirs. We faced each other across the room, unable to communicate.

I saw on Gheorghe's desk a well-worn Bible. I took my own Dutch Bible from my coat pocket and turned to 1 Corinthians 16:20.

"All the brethren greet you. Greet ye one another with an holy kiss."

I held the Bible out and pointed to the name of the book, recognizable in any language, and the chapter and verse number.

Their faces lit up.

They swiftly found the place in their own Bible, read it and beamed at me. Gheorghe thumbed the pages. He held out for me Proverbs 25:25: "As cold water to a thirsty soul, so is good news from a far country."

Now we were all three laughing. I turned to Philemon.

"I thank my God always when I remember you in my prayers, because I hear of your love and of the faith which you have toward the Lord. . . ."

It was Ion's turn. His eyes traveled over the next lines, and he pushed the Bible to me, pointing with his finger:

"For I have derived much joy and comfort from your love, my brother, because the hearts of the saints have been refreshed through you."

We had a wonderful half hour, conversing with each other through the Bible. We laughed until tears were in our eyes. And when at the end of the conversation I brought out Romanian Bibles and shoved them across the desk and insisted with gestures that, yes, they were supposed to keep them, both men embraced me.

Later that day, I made arrangements with Ion to take all the Bibles I had brought with me. He would know where to place them.

Over the next week and a half I traveled throughout Romania with an excellent interpreter, following leads given by Gheorghe and Ion.

I met every shade of attitude, from defeat to courage. It was easy to sympathize with the defeated ones. "What can we do?" was such a natural reaction. So many wanted to get out of Romania altogether.

Oddly, though, the more devoted a Christian, the more likely he was to stay put. In Transylvania we visited such a family. They had a poultry farm, but the State had given them a production quota that was beyond their capacity to meet. Year after year this happened.

"Why do you stay? To keep your farm?" I asked.

The farmer and his wife both looked shocked. "Of course not," he said. "We certainly will lose the farm. We stay because if we go, who will be left to pray?"

I also met Christians who were less sure. I visited one church that was working with gypsies. The grass was high in the churchyard, and several windows in the sanctuary were broken. My interpreter and I walked behind the church to the pastor's living quarters and knocked. The pastor was not at home, but his wife invited us inside.

She and her husband had worked among the gypsies for many years. Recently, she said, the government had decided to do something for the gypsies by offering them jobs. She and her husband had been delighted. But there was a condition: No gypsy who attended the church could apply for one of the new jobs.

"And so our members are leaving us. As our congregation dwindles, the Party has more of an argument for taking away our building. I don't think we will be here next year."

She began to cry. I suggested the three of us pray about the things she had told us. We bowed our heads, and I prayed for her and for her husband, for the gypsies, for the whole desperate situation in that village. When we raised our heads, her eyes were moist again as she said, "You know, years ago, I knew that people in the West were praying for us, but now for many years we have not heard from them. We've never been able to write letters, and it's been thirteen years since we've received one. It seems that we are forgotten."

I was able to assure her from the depth of my heart that as soon as I got back, people would know about them. They need never again feel they carried their burden alone.

For my last hours in Romania, I attended a Sunday service with Gheorghe and Ion. Gheorghe spoke for the last sermon. He talked about the shortness of breath that had plagued him for years. "But when we had that wonderful conversation with our Bibles, something happened—I've been breathing better."

Gheorghe opened his Bible. "I have a final Scripture that I should like to share with you, Andrew," he told me through the interpreter. "Will you open your Book to Acts 20:36–38?"

I found the place.

"This," said Gheorghe, "is the passage that says good-bye the way I should like to. 'And when we had spoken thus, he knelt down and prayed with them all. And they all wept and embraced Paul and kissed him, sorrowing most of all because of the words he had spoken, that they should see his face no more. And they brought him to the ship.'"

I had to laugh at him applying words about Paul to me. "That's going from the highest to the lowest," I said.

But I knelt down and prayed once more with them all. Then these Christians in the center of Communism wept, embraced me and accompanied me to my little blue ship.

16

The Work Expands

Our son Joppie arrived on June 4, 1959. He was born at home, as I had been, and I was with Corry the whole time.

With Joppie's arrival it was clear that Corry and I needed a home of our own. But the effects of war were seen in Holland, and part of that was a housing shortage.

When I went to see the burgomaster about house rentals, he shook his head. "If you could find a house to buy, that would be different. The waiting list applies only to rentals." He added, "But as far as I know, there are no houses for sale."

The clothes that people continued to send swamped our room. Every night for a week we laid our situation before God.

Then I remembered something. The schoolteacher who was moving to Haarlem—wasn't he renting old Wim's house in Witte?

The idea came to me in the sudden and sovereign manner I had come to recognize. Suppose Wim was willing to sell the house. He had not lived in it himself for many years. I was not going to think about the twenty thousand guilders it would cost. I would take a step forward and see what happened.

I struck out across the polders to Wim's farm. I found him milking.

"Hello, Wim!"

"Hello, Andrew!" Wim said. "What can I do for you?"

"I hear your place in town is going to be empty. Have you thought of selling it?"

Wim's jaw literally dropped open. "I made up my mind to sell last night—but I hadn't told a soul!"

I drew a deep breath. "Would you consider selling it to me?"

Wim looked at me for a long time. "House has been in the family many generations," he said at last. "I'd like nothing better than for it to be used for the Lord's work."

Only then did I ask the price.

"Well," Wim said, "how about ten thousand?"

That was half what I thought he might ask. "All right, Wim. We have an understanding. I will buy your house," I said, with not a penny to my name, "for ten thousand guilders."

I telephoned Mr. Whetstra. Never before in my life had I borrowed money, but it seemed to me that this was right.

Mr. Whetstra told me that if I came to his office the following day, I could have the money then and there.

By the time I returned to our room above the shed, Corry and I were the virtual possessors of a house. We went to look at it. Until then I never realized how it had been for Corry, living in someone else's home. Now she ran from room to room, touching, planning, seeing the home that was to be. "Joppie in here, Andy. And look, a whole room for the clothes, with the laundry tub right there! Did you see the room upstairs where your desk will fit?" On she went, eyes aglow.

The next day I went to Amsterdam and picked up the money. Mr. Whetstra handed it to me in cash. We signed no papers, made no payment arrangements. Nor did I mention the loan to anyone else. Yet over the next three years, enough money came in above and beyond the needs of the work that we were able to repay the loan in that short period of time. As soon as the house was paid for, the excess funds stopped—and remained dried up until there was need for them again.

That first year after Joppie's birth I revisited every country I could get back into—several more than once. As the work grew, so did the problems. Correspondence was number one. Each time I got home, I would spend miserable days pecking out on a typewriter answers to a mountain of mail. I never reached the bottom of the pile.

I stopped using my full name and began instead to use the name by which I was known behind the Curtain, where last names had ceased to exist among Christians: "Brother

Andrew." I took out a post-office box number in my brother Ben's town for inquiries about the work.*

Travel was one thing for a bachelor, quite another for a married man with a child. I missed Joppie's first tooth, first word, first step. Mr. Ringers reminded me of his standing offer of a job at the factory—at a salary that sounded kingly. I was also offered the pastorate of a church in The Hague.

Both times I was tempted, but never for long. A letter would arrive. It would bear no return address, it would often have been mailed weeks earlier and sometimes it would show signs of having been opened. It would be from some believer in Bulgaria or Hungary or Poland or elsewhere writing about new troubles, new needs. I would pack my bags again and seek a visa for travel to the world of the Communists.

In West Germany, the car engine finally breathed its last.

I was on my way home from a trip to East Germany and Poland. With me were two Dutch students who had worked in the refugee camps in Berlin. One afternoon we were spinning along, when suddenly there was a crackling sound in the rear of the car. The engine died. Nothing we could do would make it start again.

Beside the road was an emergency telephone box. I picked up the receiver and asked for a tow truck. Within twenty minutes we were all bending over the engine at the service garage.

*Brother Andrew, Open Doors, P.O. Box 47, 3840 AA Harderwijk, The Netherlands. Email brotherandrew@opendoors.org.

The manager inspected the engine, then looked at the odometer.

"Ninety-seven thousand kilometers," he read. "It's a good mileage. . . ."

I admitted that the odometer had long ago reached 99,999 and flipped over to the zero mark; this was the second time it registered 97,000.

"Then I should say you've got your money's worth," said the manager. "That engine hasn't any more to give."

"How long would it take to put in a new one?"

"My crew leaves in ten minutes. They could install a new engine in an hour, but you'd have to pay them a tip for staying overtime."

"How much would the whole thing cost, including the tip?"

"Five hundred marks."

"Go ahead," I said. "I'll get some money changed at the train station."

On the streetcar going to the station, I counted my money and realized that all I had with me would not make five hundred marks. There would be no help from the two students—they were flat broke.

Should I cancel the work order? No. I saw God's hand too clearly in this—stopping precisely at the emergency telephone, having the engine wear out here in Germany where it came from, rather than in some spot where replacement would have been impossible. I was too familiar with the way Christ looks after the practical side of ministry to miss these signs. This was His timing, and the question of the money was in His hands. I was fascinated to see how He would work it out.

When I had changed every last guilder, it came—with the German money in my pocket—to 470 marks. Fifty shy of the amount needed to pay the bill and buy gasoline on the way home.

Back at the garage the workmen finished up. My two passengers had gone for a walk, the men said.

I could delay the moment of reckoning no longer.

At that instant, the two Dutchmen raced through the door, one of them waving something in his hand. "Andy! Craziest thing ever happened!" he said. "We were walking along the street when this lady came up to us and asked if we were Dutchmen. When I said yes, she gave me this bill! She said God wanted us to have it!"

It was fifty marks.

In spite of this experience—and others like it occurring almost daily—I still depended on the isolated miracle, the emergency action to get me out of one spot or another, instead of leaning back in the arms of the Father.

Back home there were new expenses, the biggest of which was the arrival of a second baby, Mark Peter. We started buying less meat, depending more on the vegetables from our garden. This was no hardship, for we loved vegetables. What we did not realize was that it was part of a mental "attitude of lack" into which we had slipped.

It came to my attention through the words of a lady I have never met.

One day we received a gift of money, the equivalent of about forty dollars. Attached to the check was a note: *"Dear Brother Andrew: This is to be used for your own personal needs. It is* not *to go into the work! Use it in Christ's love."*

I was touched by this. We received personal gifts sometimes from friends, but this was the first time a stranger ever made such a stipulation. I wrote a thank-you that very day. I told her we appreciated the note, because this was something we were very scrupulous about: All donations went into the work unless they were specifically marked otherwise. Even our clothing, I told her, came out of the refugee bins to save money.

I wish I had saved the letter this good lady shot back. She reminded me that the Scriptures say the ox grinding the corn must not be kept from enjoying the grain. Did God feel less about His human workers? Wasn't I claiming to depend upon God, but living as if my needs would be met by my own scrimping? I remember her closing: *"God will send you what your family needs and what your work needs, too. You are a mature Christian, Brother Andrew. Act like one."*

I gave that letter a long and prayerful reading. Could she be right? Was I living in an atmosphere of want that was un-Christian?

About this time, Corry and I were invited out to dinner. The time came to leave, and Corry had not appeared. I went to our room and found her in her bathrobe.

"I have nothing to wear," she said in a small voice.

I laughed. Wasn't this what women always said?

Then I saw tears in her eyes. I looked over her wardrobe myself. Warm dresses. Serviceable ones, thanks to Corry's mending. But the clothes she had salvaged from the refugee room did not include anything pretty.

Now I saw this pattern of poverty into which we had fallen, an attitude that hardly went with the Christ of the open heart that we preached.

We changed. We still lived frugally. But at the same time we made much-needed remodeling work to the house. Corry bought some dresses. And when our third baby, Paul Denis, arrived, we actually bought him new clothes.

For years I had been working alone—traveling over eighty thousand kilometers a year, being away from home two-thirds of the time. I was prepared to do this as long as it seemed to be what God wanted. But sometimes lately, the work had suffered simply because I could not be in two places at once!

Suppose I had a partner traveling with me! Suppose there were two of us . . . three of us . . . ten! Someone to be where another could not, to spell each other with the travel, the speaking, even the letter-writing!

It would have to be an unusual fellowship. The less formally we were organized the better, so if we were arrested, we would not involve each other. We would be a small band of men and women with the same vision of bringing hope to the Church in its need.

I shared my dream with Corry, and she said, "I'll be frank, Andrew—my reaction is selfish. Do you realize your family would be able to *see* you once in a while?"

Immediately she was sorry she had said it. But I wasn't. My long absences were hard on us all. If I had help, these long trips would not be as necessary.

Fairly often, at the close of a talk, I would find three or four eager young men standing around the rostrum.

"Brother Andrew, can I join you in your work behind the Iron Curtain? God has told me, too, to preach the Gospel there." Others were probably a little more honest. "It sounds so exciting!" they would say.

I would respond, "If I meet you behind the Iron Curtain, then by all means let's talk some more."

That would be the last I would hear of them.

"If God wants to expand the work," I said to Corry one night, "He certainly has prepared the people. How do I find them?"

"Try prayer."

I laughed. That was my Corry. We prayed, then and there. Immediately a name came to mind.

Hans Gruber.

I had met Hans in Austria, working at a refugee camp. He was a giant Dutchman, six-feet-seven, heavy even for that height and awkward beyond belief. He seemed to have six elbows, ten thumbs and a dozen knees. And he spoke the most atrocious German I had ever heard.

And yet he was totally right for the mission. He could stand up in the camp and hold five hundred people spellbound hour after hour, simply with words. I had seen it begin to rain while Hans spoke, in that horrid German, without a single listener glancing at the sky. In the orphaned boys' compound he was master. This group of 240 bored, restless kids was the terror of every speaker who visited. For Hans they sat like statues and then followed him around the camp like pet sheep.

That evening I wrote Hans, asking him if he had ever felt led to bring this preaching ministry behind the Iron

Curtain. I knew, I wrote him, where my next trip would be. There was a new relaxation of travel restrictions in Russia. It was now possible for foreigners to travel in the Soviet Union on their own, without an official guide. It was time to penetrate into the heartland of Communism.

Hans's answer came back. He was ecstatic. My suggestion was for him the fulfillment of an old prophecy. When he was in the sixth grade, he had had a strange sensation every time he looked at the map of Russia, as though a voice told him, *Someday you will work for Me in that land.*

"Ever since," he wrote, "I've studied Russian to be ready when the time came. My Russian is good now—almost as good as my German. When do we go?"

Now we needed a new car. We purchased a new Opel station wagon. We could sleep in it, even Hans at his size, and we could carry many more Bibles.

Once we hit the road, I could see that Hans was in some ways miles ahead of me in trusting God with the work.

Friends we stayed with in Berlin were enthralled at the idea of taking Bibles to the Soviet Union. "Our church has some Russian Bibles! Couldn't you take them along?"

"Of course we'll take them," said Hans. "If we're going to be arrested for carrying Bibles, we might as well be arrested for carrying a lot of them."

So we squeezed the extra books in. Then as we were leaving, some other friends arrived with a carton of Ukrainian Bibles. I looked at Hans and knew that box was going with us. This time there was no storage place.

"Well," said Hans, "you say you leave a few Bibles in plain sight, so that God can do the job and not you. I'll carry these on my lap."

At the border crossing into Russia, Hans could hardly contain his excitement. He insisted on speaking Russian with the customs officials. I doubt they understood one word in ten, but they appreciated that he made the effort.

Then came time for the inspection of the car. Hans and I had agreed ahead of time on the technique we would use from then on whenever two people crossed a border together. One of us would talk; the other would be in constant prayer that God's will be done in the inspection—and prayer for the country we were entering, beginning with these employees at the border.

The guard asked us to open a couple of suitcases, but he hardly glanced inside. He wanted to see the Opel motor. He asked some technical questions, then slammed the hood shut. He stamped our papers and wished us farewell.

We were across.

At First Glance

It was Hans's first trip into Russia but not mine. I had accompanied a group of young people from the Netherlands, Germany and Denmark to a Youth Congress in Moscow, much like the one in Warsaw years before. We were gone two weeks, traveling by train and following an official schedule. As a scouting trip it had been of enormous value.

Now as Hans and I drove across the Russian landscape, from Brest to Moscow, I told him about my earlier trip.

The hotel where I was assigned was in a village eight miles outside of Moscow. That Sunday I made my way to the only Protestant church in Moscow that was still open. I expected a small and demoralized congregation.

But there was a long line of people waiting outside. A man came up and spoke to me in German.

"You've come to church?" he asked.

"Yes."

"Come. There's a balcony reserved for foreign visitors."

*From the balcony I saw for the first time the Moscow Prot-
estant Church at worship. The hall was narrow and long,
with balconies on each side, a platform seating twelve in the
front, a fine organ and a stained-glass window facing east.*

*There were close to two thousand people there that morn-
ing. Every seat was taken. The aisles were packed with
standees, and the balconies were overflowing.*

*The singing began. Two thousand Slavic voices in unison,
drowning out the organ. I could imagine I was hearing
heavenly choirs. Then there were two sermons.*

*During the sermons, the strangest thing happened. People
in the congregation made paper airplanes and sailed them
forward. No one seemed disturbed by this. The planes were
passed forward and collected by men on the platform. These,
I learned, were prayer requests.*

*The pastor held the prayer request piles high. He read
the names of visitors and said, "Are we glad to have these
visitors?"*

"Amen!"

"Do we hold them up in prayer?"

"Amen!"

*"These requests"—he read two or three notes—"Do we
pray for these needs?"*

"Amen!"

"Let us pray."

*Then that entire congregation of two thousand began to
pray aloud simultaneously. From time to time a single voice*

would rise above the sound while the other voices faded to a background hum. The tide of sound would swell again. This experience stirred me to the depths of my spirit.

After the service it was announced that the pastors would be glad to greet any visitors downstairs and answer questions. A dozen of us accepted the invitation. Questions were fired in quick succession. "Where is the next closest Protestant church?"

"Oh, there are many Protestant churches in Russia."

"Where are they?"

"Some are very near."

"Is there religious freedom in Russia?"

"We have complete religious freedom here, yes."

"How about pastors who have been jailed?"

"We know of no pastors who are in jail, except, perhaps, political subversives."

I asked my question. "Do you have enough Bibles?"

"There are plenty of Bibles, yes."

"How many?"

"Oh, lots."

On it went, questions followed by smooth answers that said nothing. The next day, hoping to see one of the pastors alone, I went back to the church. The church building also served as the central office of the Baptist Union for all of Russia.

"Can I help you?"

I turned and recognized one of the men who had answered questions the previous morning. He introduced himself as Ivanhoff and invited me into his office. I decided to start right out and tell him about the Bibles.

"I've brought something from the Baptists of Holland to the Baptists of Russia." I placed a package tied in brown paper on his table.

"What do you have there?"

"Bibles."

He seemed to be maintaining his composure with difficulty. "May I please see them?"

I untied the string and showed him the three Bibles I had brought on the train.

The pastor restrained his eagerness with great effort.

"Did you say these were a gift?"

"Yes."

Leaning forward, he said, "Tell me, my friend, why did you really come to Russia?"

I cast about for the best answer.

"Do you remember in the Bible when Joseph was wandering among the Shechemites? One of the Shechemites saw him and asked him a question. Do you remember?"

The pastor thought. "He asked, 'Whom are you seeking?'"

"And Joseph's answer?"

"He said, 'I seek my brethren.'"

"That," I said, "is my answer to your question, too."

Hans listened with great interest. At the end, he offered one of his faith-filled prayers that we be led to Ivanhoff again.

For Russia with Love

The avenues of Moscow were wide and more heavily traveled than I remembered. We drove through Red Square and on to the campsite that had been assigned to us. We pitched our tent and prepared to take out a few Bibles.

"Don't look now," Hans said, "but we've got prying eyes."

Without looking up, I tossed a road map on top of the two Bibles I had taken out. Casually I glanced around and saw the man wearing a green fatigue uniform. He stood a few feet from the car, watching us. Hans and I started preparing an unwanted cup of coffee. As soon as we stopped unpacking the Bibles, the prying eyes walked away.

We took one of the Bibles, locked the car and left the campsite. We headed for midweek service at a Baptist church.

About twelve hundred people attended this Thursday night prayer meeting! When it was over, Hans and I walked out to the vestibule and began milling about in the crowd, hoping to make contacts for delivering our Bibles. I edged my way around the entrance hall, glancing into face after face, asking God to give me, as He had so often before, that moment of recognition.

I saw a thin man in his middle forties standing against a wall and staring into the crowd. I had such a clear directive to speak to him that I almost forgot about Hans. But I waited until Hans had inched over to my side.

"I've spotted our man!" he said. Out of hundreds of people in that vestibule, he nodded to the man I had chosen. We pushed our way to him.

"Kak vi po zhi vayete," Hans began.

"Kak vi po zhi vayete," the man answered, instantly alert.

As Hans launched into a description of who we were and where we were from, however, the man's face grew more and more perplexed. But when Hans came to the word *Dutch*, he burst out laughing. He told us that he himself was German. We learned that his family were German immigrants, and they still spoke German at home.

The three of us fell into conversation. This man was from a church in Siberia, two thousand miles away, where there were 150 communicants but not a single Bible. One day he was told in a dream to go to Moscow, where he would find a Bible for his church. He resisted the idea, he said, for he knew as well as anyone that there were few Bibles in Moscow. That was the end of his story.

Hans and I looked at each other in disbelief. Then Hans spoke. "You were told to come westward two thousand miles to get a Bible, and we were told to go eastward two thousand

miles carrying Bibles to churches in Russia. Here we are tonight, recognizing each other the instant we meet."

With this, Hans held out the Russian Bible we had brought with us. The Siberian was without words. He held the Bible and stared at it, and then at the two of us, and then at the Bible again. All of a sudden the dam burst, and a flow of thank-yous and bear hugs followed. I whispered to the man that we had more Bibles. If he would meet us there at ten the next morning, we would give him more.

The next morning at nine o'clock, Hans posted guard while I tried to get Bibles out of their hiding place in the car. I was halfway through when Hans whistled the Dutch national anthem. Our friend in the green uniform was back. I started making coffee.

"Coffee's ready!" I shouted.

Hans took a cup from my hands. "He's suspicious about something. How many did you get out?"

"Four."

"That'll have to do."

Owning a Bible for your own personal use was no crime. But smuggling them in was illegal; it was dangerous to look as if you might be dealing in contraband. We put four Bibles into our flight bags and strolled to the bus stop. At precisely ten o'clock we walked into the church and sat near the door. At 10:30 we were feeling conspicuous. Then, at 10:45, a voice spoke at my elbow. "Hello, Brother."

I whirled around. It was Ivanhoff, the pastor I had met on my previous visit to Moscow.

"Are you waiting for someone?" Ivanhoff asked.

"Yes. Someone we met here last night."

Ivanhoff was silent for a moment. Then he said softly, "That's what I was afraid of. Your Siberian friend cannot come."

"What do you mean?"

Ivanhoff looked around. "My friends," he said, "at each service there are secret police. We count on it. They saw you and this man talking, so he cannot come. But you have brought something for him?"

"Yes," I said. "Four Bibles. In these bags."

"Leave them with me. I will see that he gets them."

We took the Bibles—wrapped in newspaper—out of the bags and handed them over.

"Is there somewhere we can talk?" I asked. "These aren't the only Bibles we have."

Ivanhoff caught his breath. "What do you mean? Keep your voice low. How many do you have?"

"Over a hundred. They're in our car at the camp."

Ivanhoff thought for a moment. Then he led us down a long corridor. When it turned a corner, he stopped suddenly, laid the Bibles on the floor and held out his hands, palms down.

"Do you see my nails?" he said. We stared at fingernails ridged and thickened the way nails become when they are damaged in their roots. "I have spent my time in prison for the faith. I cannot go through it again. I cannot help you with those Bibles."

My heart went out to this man. "Perhaps you know of someone else who might be willing?"

"Markov," said Ivanhoff. "I will arrange for him to meet you in front of the GUM store at precisely one o'clock." Then as an afterthought, "Be careful."

Hans pointed to the Bibles on the floor. "Don't you risk something taking these?"

Ivanhoff smiled, but his eyes remained sad. "Four Bibles," he said. "That's not a serious economic crime. They're worth four hundred rubles. You go to jail four months at the most for four hundred rubles. But a hundred Bibles! That's worth ten thousand rubles in Moscow. Why, a man could—"

He stopped talking, snatched the books from the floor and walked rapidly away.

That afternoon at one o'clock we pulled up in front of the GUM department store. A man emerged from a car parked a hundred yards away. He strolled by, looking at us cautiously through the window. Then he strolled back again.

"Brother Andrew?"

"You're Markov," I said. "Greetings in the name of the Lord."

"We're going to do something very bold," said Markov, talking rapidly. "We're going to exchange the Bibles within two minutes of Red Square. No one will suspect us in such a location."

He led us to a street that was, sure enough, less than two minutes from Red Square. There was a large blind wall running along one side of the street, but houses lined the other.

"You'd better pray," I said to Hans as I parked behind Markov's car.

Hans did pray, aloud, as I got the Bibles and stowed them into cartons and sacks. Markov opened the rear door to his car, and we made the transfer right out in the open on the busy sidewalk. When we finished, Markov gave a quick handshake before he was back in his car starting the engine.

"By next week," he said, "these Bibles will be in the hands of pastors all over Russia."

As Markov drove off, I looked at Hans. He was grinning. Except for one carton of Ukrainian Bibles, the car was empty.

We went home by way of the Ukraine, delivering the last Bibles to churches ourselves. A parishioner brought something for us to see—his family's pocket-sized Ukrainian Bible.

I held the little volume in my hand, unbelieving. Yes, the man assured me, it was a complete Bible. It was one quarter the size of the Bibles we had brought! I turned the pages, marveling at the tiny type, so small and yet so sharp, each word clear and well-spaced. I bombarded the man with questions—where had this been printed, who published it, where had they bought it? He didn't know.

I could not lay the little book down. I hefted it in my hand. I slipped it into my pocket. I held it up beside one of the standard Bibles. We could bring in three and four times as many, every trip, if they were this size! If it could be done for Ukrainian, Russian could be printed in this format, too, and the other Eastern European languages. . . .

The owner made a suggestion. If he could have two new ones we had brought, would we like to keep this one? The church would still be one Bible ahead.

I left that town with a dream in my pocket. I could hardly wait to show it to our Bible societies in the West.

Our last Sunday in Russia we attended a Baptist church in a Ukrainian village. When it came time for the sermon, the pastor borrowed a Bible from someone in the congregation. We had heard about ministers in Russia who did not have Bibles of their own. This was the first time we saw it.

After the service the pastor invited us to join him and his elders in his study for a brief visit. We talked about the Second Coming of Christ—the most popular theological topic in Russia at the time. I drew my Dutch Bible out of my pocket to follow the references being made and then laid it on the desk.

The pastor lost interest in the conversation. His mind was on the Bible! He picked it up and weighed it in his hand, unzipped the cover, stared at the Dutch words he could not read, zipped it up again.

He put it back on the desk with great precision. He set it down on the corner and slowly ran his finger along the edge so that it was aligned with the desk. Then he said, "You know, Brother, I have no Bible."

My heart broke. Here was the spiritual leader of a thousand souls who did not own a copy of the Bible.

All the ones we brought with us were gone—and then I remembered. The Ukrainian pocket Bible! I raced outside to my car, got the little Bible from under the seat and ran back to the study.

I shoved the Bible into the pastor's hand. "This is for you."

"Whose is it?" he said.

"It's yours! To keep."

When Hans and I left that day, our chests ached from the embraces of that group of elders. Now their pastor had a Bible.

Bibles to the Russian Pastors

The need for a Russian pocket Bible became an obsession with me. I made the rounds of the Bible societies, but even when a society agreed that such an edition was possible, there were too many practical problems.

"Why don't you print your own pocket Bible?" said Mr. Whetstra when I talked it over with him. "You know what you want. Print it yourself."

"That would cost at least five thousand dollars. Where would I get five thousand dollars?"

Mr. Whetstra looked at me sadly. "After all this time, you ask that?"

Of course. It would not be I who supplied the funds for such a project; it would be the Lord. So I launched into another grand experiment, though this time it took longer for the dream to unfold.

Meanwhile, there was the usual work to be done. Having Hans as partner was even better than I had imagined. We formed a team, one strong where the other was weak.

In Bulgaria one night in 1962, I was writing a letter home when Hans said, "Andrew, it is time we prayed for a new team member. You remember when the visa came through to go to Czechoslovakia, only you were in East Germany and I was in Russia? If there were more of us, we wouldn't have to make these choices."

I put down my pen. "We have more opportunity than we can satisfy. That's true, Hans. But you know how it is if you expand too rapidly."

Hans interrupted. "I'd hardly call one new member in seven years expanding too rapidly. Let's pray."

I bowed my head, and as Hans spoke, I began to get his sense of urgency about finding another man who would give himself with us—full time, without salary, without reservation.

Almost simultaneously, Hans and I thought of the same person.

"What about Rolf?" we said together and then laughed.

Rolf was a young Dutch seminary student and a brilliant theologian. Also, Rolf was a man of action. Immediately I composed a letter asking him if he would consider joining us.

On our return to Holland there was a reply waiting. He said God had thrust my letter under his nose night and day until he had given in. When could he start?

So a third member joined us. Hans took him on an orientation trip into Romania. They had a fantastic time. They were spied upon by two men who hardly ever left their

sight, but in spite of this managed to get rid of their Bibles and even do some preaching in private homes.

Rolf came back utterly convinced.

We shared with Rolf our longing for a small-format Russian Bible. Rolf echoed Mr. Whetstra's thought that we should print the Bibles ourselves.

We contacted printing houses in the Netherlands, Germany and England. An English printer said he would print the Bibles for three dollars each. For a print run of five thousand copies, that came to fifteen thousand dollars!

That night I sat down at the kitchen table with a bankbook open in front of me. It was labeled "Russian Bibles." The entries, starting in 1961 just after our return from Russia, were now well into 1963. The total came to less than two thousand dollars.

Corry sat down. "What are you thinking, Andy?"

I shoved the account book toward her. "In two years that's all the money we've saved." I hated saying what I had to next. "How much do you think our house is worth?"

Corry stared at me. "Our *house*? Right when we're expecting a new baby?" Her face went white. "Maybe God doesn't want us to have those pocket Bibles," she said in a small voice. "Maybe the very slowness is guidance."

That was all we said that night about selling the house. But Corry told me the next week that she had begun to pray that she could think of the house as belonging to God.

"It should be Yours to do with as You will," we started praying together. "And yet we know we really don't feel this way, Lord. If You want us to sell the house for the Bibles, You will have to make us willing."

The new baby came—a little girl we named Stephanie.

We now asked God to make us *willing* to be *willing* to sell the house.

He answered our prayer. One morning Corry and I suddenly knew that we didn't need that house or anything else on earth to make us happy.

"I don't know where we'll live." Corry laughed. "Remember, Andy? 'We don't know where we're going—'"

I supplied the end of the sentence, "'—but we're going there together.'"

That day we got an appraisal on the house and land. The total, coupled with our savings account, came to just over fifteen thousand dollars!

It was the confirmation we needed. We put the house on the market, and I wrote to the printer in England, asking him to start the work we had discussed. That night Corry and I slept better than we had in months.

God asks for so little in order to give us so much. For although the housing shortage in Witte was still acute, not a single person came to look at our house all that week.

On Friday, the Dutch Bible Society called, asking to see me that afternoon.

Soon I was seated across the table from the board of directors. They had not been able to get my need out of their minds, so here was what they proposed. They would pay half the cost of printing the Bibles. If the Bibles cost $3 each to print, I could purchase them for $1.50. And although the Society would pay for the entire printing as soon as it was ready, I would need to pay for my supplies only as I used them.

I could scarcely believe it. I would be able to buy over six hundred Bibles—all we could carry at one time—right away out of our Russian Bible fund. We would not have to sell our home. I could hardly wait to tell Corry what God did with the thimbleful of willingness we offered Him.

The pocket Bibles were a reality at last. Within six months we would begin supplying Russian pastors with the Bibles they so desperately needed.

Rolf was getting married.

Corry and I had dutifully told him the disadvantages and separations that went with this type of work. But as Rolf pointed out, our own happiness was the best argument against bachelorhood. Elena could go with him on his trips. She would be just as effective a team member as the men.

So we stood up for them at their wedding and gave them a honeymoon assignment. The first print order of Bibles was ready. Rolf and Elena would go pick them up in England.

We had a second vehicle now, a van for long-distance travel. It had a windowless rear section and could carry more than the Opel could. Rolf and his bride drove the van to England and picked up our first order of pocket Bibles. What a red-letter day it was when they burst into the house carrying one of the new Bibles, our own edition! I knew that we must be on our way to Russia. Hans was in Hungary, so newlywed Rolf was tapped.

It was Sunday morning in Moscow, time to go downtown to church. Rolf and I left the van with considerable uneasiness. This cargo represented a sizable smuggling operation in cash value alone. We were giving the Bibles away, but that would make no difference if we were caught with them. It would be an "economic crime" against the State. A man convicted of the same charge had recently been executed by firing squad. If we were caught . . . well, this was not the time to think of that.

Ivanhoff was on the platform at church that morning. As he glanced at the visitors' balcony, I was sure he recognized me, although he gave no sign. A few minutes later he got up and left. He did not return, nor was he in the vestibule after the service. But a hearty voice behind me said, "Welcome to Russia!"

It was Markov. I introduced him to Rolf. "We brought gifts," I said.

"Wonderful!" he cried. His voice was louder than necessary, and I knew it was a defense. No one would bother to listen if we were speaking openly.

"I wonder where we might go to visit."

"How about the same place as before?"

Two minutes from Red Square! Markov had nerves of steel, but I did not.

"I'd rather see some new scenery."

Markov lowered his voice. "On the road to Smolensk there is a large blue sign saying 'Moscow.' Rendezvous there at five o'clock. I will lead you to another place. Have the gifts unpacked so we can move fast."

Where to unpack those Bibles? It would take half an hour of privacy to do the job.

"Let's go for a ride," I said to Rolf. "I'll crawl into the back and begin unpacking. Whatever you do, keep moving."

I had barely begun when the van jerked to a halt. I peered over the seats. A police officer was approaching the car.

"Pray!" Rolf hissed, and then stuck his head out the window. "What is it, officer?" he asked in Dutch.

The policeman rattled off a long angry sentence in Russian, then produced a few words in English. "No turn! No turn! Sign say."

"I'm terribly sorry," said Rolf, still in Dutch.

I flattened my back against the side of the van, praying the officer would not look inside. At the end of a lifetime he said something else in Russian, more calmly. "The same to you, officer," Rolf answered in Dutch.

Rolf put the van into gear and moved slowly out into traffic. Several blocks later, I exhaled.

"Why are we worried?" Rolf said suddenly. "This is God's work! He'll make a way for us." As if to prove his conviction, he started to sing.

Oddly, as the mood inside the van brightened, the sky overhead darkened. First clouds hid the sun, and then clouds spread across the sky, dark and threatening. Lightning flashed in the distance. Thunder answered.

Then the rain began.

I had never seen rain like this. It was a solid sheet of water. We had to pull to the side of the road. Other cars, too, had to abandon the road. The windows steamed up. "God has made us invisible!" said Rolf.

We crawled back into the van and packed the Bibles into cartons. We settled back in our seats as the rain lifted.

At five o'clock we drove past the Moscow sign. Markov passed us, his headlights on. He blinked them once. Ten minutes later, we stopped in front of a shopping center where people all around us were unloading boxes or piling them into trucks. It took five minutes to make the exchange.

The Awakening Dragon

ne day in Moscow I sat on a bus next to a Chinese man. There were hundreds of Chinese in Moscow in those days, but this man wore a cross in his lapel. We got to talking, in English, and he told me he was indeed a Christian and also the secretary of the Shanghai YMCA. He gave me his card and invited me to visit.

From that day on, a hope-beyond-hope began to grow within me of someday ministering to the Christians of China.

But how many Christians were in China, anyhow? I knew the majority of the population never had been Christian. On the other hand, China had seen many missionaries. Were the congregations they founded still functioning? Were they meeting in secret? If they still existed, were they as hungry for Bibles as the churches in Eastern Europe?

When a speaking tour took me to California in 1965, I decided to keep going, to visit Taiwan to talk with people who knew China, and then to try to get onto the mainland itself. I was counting on my Dutch passport—Dutchmen sometimes were still permitted to travel behind that stronger-than-iron curtain.

On the plane to Hong Kong, I discovered I had started out all wrong. The man next to me, a Hong Kong banker, looked at me oddly when I told him I was bound for China. "Didn't you get aboard at Taiwan?" he said.

"Yes, I spent ten days there."

"Let me see your passport." He flipped through the pages looking for the Taiwan stamp but stopped at the American visa. "United States!" he said.

"Yes. I've just come from there."

"You'll never get into Red China with that passport."

Usually I enjoy it when people tell me something is impossible, because this allows me to experience God's way of dealing with impossibilities. But no sooner had I checked in at the Hong Kong YMCA than I began to hear more discouraging facts. Hong Kong was full of missionaries—including doctors and teachers with records of service—who had tried and failed to get into mainland China. The fact that they had been accredited under the pre-Communist regime automatically barred them from the country.

I went to the Dutch consulate. When I told the consul I wanted to go to the China mainland, he began to smile. When I explained I was a missionary, his smile broadened. When I told him I wanted to look for Christians there and bring Bibles to them, he began to laugh.

"May I see your passport?" he said. He ruffled through the pages, shaking his head. "Impossible," he said.

"Sir," I said, "that's why I'm here. I want a new passport."

"Impossible," he said again. The consulate in Hong Kong had no authority to issue passports. If he were to send my request higher, he would have to show legal cause, and there was none. The interview was over.

At first I was disappointed; then suddenly I was glad. There was no possibility of getting into China by my own cleverness. I believed the desire to go to China had come from God; I would leave the means to Him. The next morning I would go to the Chinese consulate and apply for a visa, knowing that if God wanted me to go, the necessary papers would be forthcoming.

I set out in search of the Chinese "travel agency," as the tourism department of that government was called. When I found it, it was closed. On the sidewalk in front of the barred door, I began to pray, binding any force that could prevent me from going where God willed, proclaiming the fact that Christ had been victorious over any power opposed to the rule of God. Back and forth in front of the building I walked and prayed for two hours.

The next morning I was back. This time the door was open. I walked into a large room jammed with people. I chose a line, waited and prayed. When it was my turn, I stepped forward. The man in the pale blue uniform looked up at me inquiringly.

"Sir," I said in English, "I want to make application for a visa to China."

"Have you ever been to the United States or to Taiwan?" he asked.

"Yes, sir. I've just come from Taiwan, and before that I was in California."

"Then," he said, "you cannot go to China, because these countries are our enemies."

"But," I said, smiling, "they are not my enemies, for I have no enemies. Will you give me the forms?"

We held each other's eye. He looked at me without expression for a time. At last his gaze broke. "It will achieve nothing," he said with a shrug. But he handed me the application forms. He told me the application, with my passport, would have to travel up to Canton and that I would hear back after three days.

That night I had dinner with a missionary. "They said I might hear after three days!" I told him jubilantly.

My host laughed. "They always say that. Three days is Chinese for never."

For those three days I fasted and prayed constantly. I went to the local Bible shop and purchased supplies of Chinese Scripture to take with me behind the Bamboo Curtain. And I waited.

On the third day I returned to my room at the YMCA to find a note telling me to telephone the Chinese travel agency. Instead I went directly to the office. When I reached the counter, I was silently handed my passport; attached to it was a piece of paper, stamped with the all-important visa for travel in China.

The next morning I was aboard a train to the border. This would be a two-hour trip to the town of Lo Wu. There, over a railroad bridge, was the entrance to the land of the awakening dragon.

At long last the British customs officer told us we could cross the bridge. We walked single file. At the halfway point the shade of green in which the girders were painted changed. We were in Communist China.

On this side of the border was a large complex of buildings, neat and dull, the monotony broken by geraniums planted everywhere. The customs inspector said, "Will you please open your valise?"

My heart beat faster. Inside, without any effort to hide them, I had put the supply of Chinese Bibles with which I would test China's reaction to the presence of a missionary.

I raised the lid to my suitcase, revealing the stacks of Bibles. The customs officer did not touch a thing. She looked at the Bibles for a moment, then raised her eyes. "Are you carrying a watch? Do you have a camera?"

No reaction at all. Was it possible she had never seen a Bible?

During my stay in China, I visited six communes. The first numbered more than ten thousand people. Here I had my first chance to visit a Chinese home—a small, thatch-roofed house on a side street. I was allowed to drop in unannounced. An old man and his wife showed us around with ever-present smiles. Pride was obvious. They pointed several times to their grain bin made of bamboo and filled with wheat. I asked through the interpreter if mice were a problem. The old man laughed.

"We have mice," he said, "but now there is enough for us and them, too. It wasn't like that 'Before.'" Everywhere I went in China, people made comparisons between "Before" the Chinese Communist Revolution and "After."

At another commune, I was shown through a hospital that, had it been in the Netherlands, would have been the last place we would have shown visitors. The operating room had neither overhead lighting nor sterilizing pan, the pharmacy was a row of empty shelves and in some of the wards the beds not only lacked sheets but mattresses, too. Yet I was shown this place as though it represented an advance.

Was this a glimpse of Before?

In Shanghai I wanted to find the YMCA secretary I had met on the bus in Moscow. I learned that the Y was still open. When I got there, through my interpreter I asked for my friend.

No one had heard of him.

"Would you mind checking?" I said. The receptionist disappeared for a while and came back with the news that no one was familiar with the name. "How can that be!" I insisted. "This man was your secretary here. Would you mind asking again?"

The receptionist stayed away for a long while. When she returned, she was smiling. "I'm sorry," she said, and then she used a phrase I was to hear often in China when I was looking for a particular person. "Your friend is not here. He is out of town."

I could only imagine why this Christian leader had vanished. How many Christians in China today were permanently "out of town"?

The secretary had told me that there was a Bible shop open in Shanghai. I found it: a small store on an out-of-the-way street, but open for business and well stocked with all sizes of Bibles. Anyone in Shanghai could buy Bibles—books that had to be smuggled into so much of Eastern Europe!

The manager spoke English and showed me around the store with pride.

I picked up a Bible from a table. To my surprise, I read in English that the book had been printed in Shanghai.

"Printed here?" I said.

"In China," the manager said proudly, "we make everything ourselves."

I had been in the store an hour, and not a single other person had come in. I asked about that.

"Not many customer," he said sadly.

How many Bibles did he sell in a month?

"Not many."

The government allowed this shop to sell its antiques because it represented no danger.

I considered my experiences trying to hand out Bibles in China. I had offered the first one to my interpreter in Canton. She handed it back; she had no time for reading. Thinking perhaps it was dangerous to be seen accepting a Bible, I tried leaving them behind "accidentally" in hotel rooms as I checked out. Before I got off the floor, the chambermaid would run after me, Bible in hand. "Please, belong you?"

I tried giving Bibles away on the street. My guides made no objection. Person after person stopped to see what I was offering, then handed the book back to me.

Now this store. "Not many customer."

I left that open, well-stocked Bible shop more discouraged than at any time since I had been in China. Persecution is an enemy the Church has met and mastered many times. Indifference could be far more dangerous.

How much can you learn about a country in a single superficial visit hampered by a language barrier and by interpreters who, you know, want you to see only the best? Impressions, perhaps, are all you take away. Many impressions were positive. The cleanliness. The absence of beggars. Some of the impressions were sad. Enormous, fully staffed dining rooms where I was the only customer. The empty streets where my taxi was the only motor vehicle in sight, yet traffic police held up pedestrians blocks ahead in preparation for the rare approach of an automobile.

Some impressions were terrifying. The morning I was leaving Nanking on the early flight, I was dressing in my hotel room when I heard shouts from the street. I ran to the window. In the square below, hundreds of men, women and children were executing a military drill. At this hour, before factories and schools opened, the entire population turned out to march, to shout, to lunge and to perform a series of high-precision maneuvers.

My taxi drove through the exercises. As we reached the corner, a command was given to "Freeze!"—a maneuver in which each person froze in the position he happened to be in, legs in midstride, arms outstretched. All those arms seemed stretched at me, fingers pointing.

In the airplane I tried to shake off the impression. But I remembered the words of a commune leader when I asked if I might see his church.

"In the communes, sir," he had said proudly, "you will find no churches. Religion is for the helpless. In China we are not helpless anymore."

I left China deeply distressed. I found one ray of hope in the disregard with which the government held the Scriptures. They apparently made no effort to prevent them from being brought into the country, sold and even printed there. Clearly they underestimated the Bible, and this might be God's opportunity. Hadn't I myself been converted simply by reading this book?

But in addition, the Holy Spirit needed dedicated, impassioned men and women in China. Even a superficial visit showed me these could not be Westerners. To minister to the Chinese today, God needed Chinese hands and voices.

21

Apostles of Hope

It was clear that we needed more team members. We aimed to revisit each Communist land at least once a year and ideally more often. We preferred to go in pairs, having found that this was so much better.

Almost every time one of us spoke, someone offered himself for our work. To weed out the novelty seekers I said, "As soon as your own ministry of encouragement is started behind the Curtain, get in touch with us and let's see if we can work together."

Once, this actually happened. I received a letter from a young Dutchman named Marcus. "I wonder if you remember the speech you gave to Swansea Bible College in Wales," he wrote. "You said, 'When you start working behind the Iron Curtain, we can talk about working together.' So let's have that talk." The letter was postmarked Yugoslavia.

"Look at this!" I said to Corry. She read the letter, too. We decided that if he got in touch with us again, we should take his suggestion seriously.

Several months later we heard from Marcus again. He was back in Yugoslavia on a second trip. The third time he wrote from Yugoslavia, he said he wanted to see us.

One day Joppie ran into my study.

"Marcus is here, Papa."

I liked Marcus the moment I saw him. Over coffee, he told us about his experiences in Yugoslavia. He had gone in with a supply of literature, which he had put on store counters or on park benches. Then he stood nearby while people helped themselves.

"I'll let you take a trip with Rolf," I said. "He'll introduce you to some pastors and church members. Get them talking, Marcus. Then come back and tell me whether you still want to work with us."

For three weeks Rolf and Marcus traveled around Yugoslavia and Bulgaria. When they returned, I did not need to ask Marcus whether or not he wanted to be part of this ministry. I could see the answer in his face.

"I had no idea," was all he said.

At last the day came when we entered the most tightly controlled Communist country of them all—Albania. It was difficult to get into, and once in, we needed all the optimism we could muster not to give up altogether.

I was away in Siberia when our group at last got its chance to enter this country. A French tourist agency arranged a two-week Albanian tour. Rolf and Marcus joined the tour as "teachers" from the Netherlands.

They carried no Bibles with them; no Albanian Bible existed. Worse, there was no one official Albanian language. In this small country, three languages or dialects were spoken: Skchip, Gheg and Tosk. The only Bibles in the country were in Latin, in Roman Catholic churches, and in Greek, in Orthodox churches. The rest of the country was Muslim.

Rolf and Marcus carried in tracts and portions of Scripture in all three Albanian languages. The customs officials at the airport did not even open their suitcases. There was a strict law in Albania forbidding the importation of any printed matter, so when Rolf and Marcus checked into their hotel with all of it untouched, they felt encouraged.

For the entire two-week trip they tried to give away those portions of Scripture. The reaction of the people was to clasp both hands behind their backs. They would not touch them. Even a Catholic bishop, to whom Rolf tried to give a Saint John's gospel, turned and stalked away down the aisle of his cathedral as though he had been offered poison.

They left a pile of tracts on a windowsill in a street of offices, thinking passersby would pick them up. A day later, two policemen arrived where the tour group was having lunch and demanded to know who had left those tracts. Marcus and Rolf confessed and had to swear they would stop such "political" activity. None of the tracts had been taken.

In terms of any future literature work in Albania, the trip was discouraging. They did learn, however, that one of the Greek Orthodox churches had a Bible in a new united Albanian language!

Marcus and Rolf requested a visit to this church. The Orthodox priest greeted them and their guide graciously. Yes, there was a brand-new translation on the high altar of the church.

He led the way down the nave of the ancient basilica. They could see the Book on the altar, an enormous volume studded with jewels. Four yards from the altar, the priest stopped—so abruptly that Rolf bumped against him. For several moments the four stood in silence, gazing at the treasure before them. When the priest turned to go, Rolf said, "May I look at it? I mean, see the pages?"

The priest's eyes widened in horror. No un-ordained person ever stood closer than four yards to the Holy Scriptures!

Then what was the sense of the new translation if it could not be read?

Why, to be carried in solemn process, the priest answered. To receive the adulation of the people. What else would a Bible be used for?

Our work in the rest of Europe was gaining momentum. Each month we made more trips than the month before. The danger of being recognized also increased.

Rolf and Elena, on a trip to Russia in 1966, had our closest call yet. They were carrying a large cargo of Bibles in the Opel. Corry and I prayed with them all night long before they left.

"Remember," I said, "your motive is love. Recognize how weak you are . . . so weak that you must depend totally upon the Spirit of God."

Our premonitions of trouble were correct. As they neared the border, they saw not one but six security officers waiting for them. Rolf told Elena to pray that God would confuse these men's thinking. "Don't stop until they're through, Elena."

They pulled up to the stop line. *"Dah zvi dahnya!"* said Rolf heartily. He chatted casually about the honeymoon they were having, visiting a number of East European countries.

"This is not the first time, either," said the officer. He read from a piece of paper all the cities Rolf and I had visited on our last trip to Russia.

This really shook Rolf.

The inspection seemed to last for hours. Two officers poked into every corner of the station wagon on the inside, while three others spent their time on the outside . . . the motor, the tires, the hubcaps. They rolled windows up and down to see if they stuck halfway. They thumped the paneling.

All the while Elena prayed. *"Confuse their thinking. . . ."*

One officer took no part in the inspection but spent the entire time scrutinizing the faces of Rolf and Elena, watching for signs that showed guilt.

Finally the inspection stopped for lack of anywhere else to look. The man with the piece of paper walked up to Rolf. "You were in Russia a few weeks ago. Tell me, why do you take frequent trips into our country?"

"My friend and I had such a wonderful time in your country that I decided to bring my bride here. And there's another reason. We have a love for the Russian people."

The officer stared at Rolf. But they had found nothing in the car, so with obvious reluctance, he signaled the car on.

As they drove away from the border, Rolf and Elena laughed and cried at the same time. Safe and secure in their station wagon were hundreds of Bibles.

One year after he joined us, Marcus, too, got married. Now we were seven: Corry and I, Rolf and Elena, Marcus and Paula, and bachelor Hans. Then Klaas and Eduard and their wives came to be part of our work.

Eduard said, "I would like to help with the correspondence." Talking rapidly as if to persuade me, he said, "I am precise and accurate, and it's the kind of work I love. Do you think there is any chance I could help you in the office?"

I looked at Corry. She was having a hard time keeping a straight face. Letters were stacked so high that a coffee cup had been missing beneath them for weeks. God handed the solution to us without our even asking for it.

The work moves on, always changing, always new. Not all of the change is good. Where there is a loosening of restrictions here, there is a tightening there. But God is never defeated. Every day we see fresh proof that indeed all things—even evil ones—work together for those who are called by His name.

And the stories go on. Here is one more.

A Romanian priest whom we helped buy Bibles for years was on his way home from Vienna, his car loaded with Bibles. He was stopped at his own border and his cargo discovered.

The priest had been in jail once on a trumped-up charge of hoarding. But here was a serious economic crime, and he was guilty. A Bible cost a month's wages in Romania, and he was carrying nearly two hundred.

Just then another car pulled up to the border. Out stepped a businessman who was well known at the station. He greeted each guard by name and walked into the inspection shed. At the sight of the counter ten-deep in Bibles, he stopped. "Bibles?" he said. "Would you be willing to sell them to me? They are confiscated, right?"

"Yes, they are confiscated, but we cannot sell them to you."

The businessman winked. "Not even for . . ." and he leaned over and whispered to the customs man. The official's eyes widened.

"Are they worth that much?"

"More. I shall make a profit."

The three guards huddled together. Apparently the price was high enough to be worth the sacrifice of principle. The businessman paid them in cash, got the priest's help loading his car with the Bibles and drove on to Romania.

There was an awkward silence. "Am I still charged with smuggling Bibles?" the priest asked.

"What Bibles?" said the customs official. "There are no Bibles here. Move along while the gate's open."

The Bibles reached Romania safely. Although they went on the black market, believers would find enough money to buy them for their own.

After decades, the mission continues.

"Where will it end?" I asked Corry one day. "Where could such a flood of caring be stopped?"

"I don't know," she said, and she laughed. "We don't know what lies ahead. We don't know where we're going but—"

"But we're glad we're going there together."

Together, the two of us. Twelve of us. Thousands of us. None of us knows where the road will lead. We only know it is the most exciting journey of them all.

EPILOGUE

The Further Adventures
of God's Smuggler

BY AL JANSSEN

rother Andrew's story did not end with the publi-
cation of *God's Smuggler*. But publicity because of
the book prevented him from traveling to Communist countries for many years. He started traveling to the
Middle East and discovered a Church struggling under
the dominance of Islam.

From 1975 to 1990 a brutal civil war raged in Lebanon.
Brother Andrew visited Christians there twice a year. During that period he began to meet with leaders of various
Islamic groups, including some who were considered terror-
ists. To his surprise he discovered that, when approached

with respect, even the most radical Muslim leaders are willing to talk with Christians.

Over the next two decades Brother Andrew sought to gain the release of hostages held by Hezbollah, a radical group funded by Iran. He visited a camp in southern Lebanon populated by leaders of Hamas, a Palestinian group whose goal is the destruction of Israel. And he preached at one of the most radical *madrasas* (Islamic schools), where the Taliban was born.

Why did Andrew go to those considered the enemies of Christians? "The best thing we can do is win our enemies to Christ," he says. "But to do that, you need to become friends. You can never win an enemy to Christ. As long as we see any person as an enemy—whether Communist, Muslim or terrorist—then the love of Christ cannot flow through us to reach them."

Along the way Brother Andrew has experienced heartbreak. He spoke at a pastors' conference in Pakistan with Haik Hovsepian, a pastor who shared the Gospel boldly all over Iran. At the end of the conference, Haik told Andrew, "When they kill me, it will not be for being silent." Two weeks later he was martyred.

In 2017 Brother Andrew turned 89. He no longer travels, but his work continues. Open Doors, the ministry he started, serves Christians who endure persecution for their faith.

Brother Andrew offers this challenge: "When we hear about terrorist attacks and read about the conflicts in Iraq and Syria and elsewhere, we must realize that the battle is first of all spiritual. The devil will do everything possible to thwart the advance of God's Kingdom. Jesus told us that if the world hated Him, it will also hate us. So we must not be surprised by the increase in persecution around the world.

"However, we are not weak. There is much we can do, starting on our knees. I can still pray. I pray that young people will accept the challenge of Jesus to *go* and make disciples in all nations. I hope that my life demonstrates that there is no more exciting mission than following Jesus wherever He leads us."

Brother Andrew is the founder of Open Doors, an international ministry to the persecuted Church and believers throughout the world. He is the author of several books, including the bestselling *God's Smuggler*, *Secret Believers* and *Light Force*. Learn more at www.opendoorsUSA.org.

Elizabeth and John Sherrill met as young people on board the *Queen Elizabeth* and were married in Switzerland. Together they have written more than thirty books, including *The Cross and the Switchblade* with David Wilkerson and *The Hiding Place* with Corrie ten Boom. The Sherrills' writing has taken them to five continents, reporting the Holy Spirit's awe-inspiring deeds in the 21st century.